MODERN ECONOMICS SERIES

Consulting Editor

PROCTER THOMSON

John C. Lincoln Professor
of Economics and Administration
Claremont Men's College

ACCOUNTING
for
Management Decisions

ACCOUNTING
for
Management Decisions

GEORGE GIBBS

Professor of Accounting and Economics
Claremont Men's College
Claremont, California

Formerly President
California State Board of Accountancy

INTERNATIONAL TEXTBOOK COMPANY
Scranton, Pennsylvania

Standard Book Number 7002 2221 9

Library of Congress Catalog Card Number: 76-76398

Preface

The accounting profession has expanded its activities in many ways in recent years. These include assisting management before a decision is made, being part of the management team which makes the decisions, and accounting for the decision after it is made.

As these activities have expanded, the concept of the accountant has broadened from the image of the stoop-shouldered man with the green eyeshade to an active member of the management team.

This book discusses the usefulness of these activities, in nontechnical language, including the management aspects of the three major segments of the economic system, namely the private, the government, and the tax-exempt. It will also outline briefly the relation of accounting principles to economic theory and policy, and consider the usefulness to management of the related studies of politics, statistics, computer applications, marketing, finance, and law.

The integration of accounting and economics in this book will be helpful to students of elementary economics and accounting, to those studying management, who may see how their interest relates to the accounting process, and to the businessman who makes decisions based on accounting data.

A decision has been defined as the act of determining in one's own mind upon an opinion or a course of action. Thus the "one" of one's own mind is important in this process. In a privately owned business it is the owner who, within the limits of the law and market behavior, personally makes decisions. In a partnership of two or more persons, each partner in the organization has the additional responsibility to his partners. The officers of the corporation have a responsibility to elected directors and to the stockholders, and, in some cases, to the general public. The decisions of the management of certain firms can affect the entire economy. (These are said to be monopolistic or oligopolistic firms, in the language of economists.)

In government the management is responsible to the elected officials and they in turn to the electorate. Thus in a democracy the accountability in government is ultimately to the members of the electorate. The final written reports of the activity of government, local, state, and Federal must be understandable by *each and every voter*! This is seldom so, but the reports of several jurisdictions have been improved recently.

The law of California is a good example of this principle of responsibility when it states that

> The people of this state do not yield their sovereignty to the agencies which serve them. The people, in delegating authority, do not give their public servants the right to decide what is good for the people to know and what is not good for them to know. The people insist on remaining informed so they may retain control over the instruments they have created.
>
> Preamble, Ralph M. Brown Act, 1953[1]

In the tax-exempt segment, the responsibility of the managers to the donors is equally strong, but these donors who are entitled to reports often do not receive any. Even the few reports that are rendered are often useless.

Since tax-exempt organizations are granted their exemption by one of the states, they are indirectly responsible to the voters of that state. However, if the organizations are not required to publish a report, and if they do not voluntarily publish one, even the most inquisitive citizen cannot easily find out what goes on. These organizations—including churches, colleges, schools, hospitals, foundations, and homes for the aged—have self-perpetuating boards of directors. Because of this and the lack of supervision by government, which granted them the exemptions from taxes, these boards begin to think that they have total responsibility and are not accountable to the voters.

My good wife Margaret C. K. Gibbs, member of the City Council of Claremont and of many other government and tax-exempt organizations, has been tolerant of the time spent on these ideas and has helped to put them in readable form. Javad Khalilzadeh-Shirazi of Meshed, Iran, a student at Claremont Men's College, and my son-in-law Claude Herbert Gengoux of Grenoble, France, have assisted by reviewing the manuscript. Mrs. Wayne R. Scherer, Faculty Secretary, and Mrs. Russell L. Folds have been indefatigable typists. However, any errors are the sole responsibility of the author.

George Gibbs

Claremont, California
January, 1969

[1] Government Code of the State of California, Sec. 54950.

Contents

PART I ACCOUNTING, WEALTH, AND INCOME

PART II VALUES AND EFFICIENCY

PART III ACCOUNTING TECHNIQUES AND TACTICS

PART IV TAXES

List of Tables

List of Figures

ACCOUNTING
for
Management Decisions

ACCOUNTING, WEALTH, AND INCOME

Chapter 1

Where Is Accounting Useful as a Tool?

Accountants assist management by gathering information on people, things, and dollars and by preparing this data in summary form for analysis. This analysis, by the projection of past data, gives some clue as to the future. It has to involve many assumptions, that are studied in economic theory.

HOW DOES THE PRIVATE SEGMENT FUNCTION?

The private segment consists of business firms, with owners, managers, employees, and customers. In smaller firms the owners and the managers are the same people. In the larger corporate enterprises, the owners may live all over the world, with the managers in one central location and the employees at various branches.

The owners of the firms in the private segment attempt to maximize their profit, that is, increase "revenue" or what comes in and decrease "expenses" or what goes out wherever possible. Each firm is said by the economists to be in an "industry" and the degree of competition within that industry ranges from relatively "pure" competition, as discussed in 1776 by Adam Smith in the *Wealth of Nations*, to monopoly, as in the case of one telephone company in a given area. In between are various degrees of "monopolistic competition" which have a bearing on this book and will be discussed later.

The private segment is not as entirely "free" of government control as the laissez-faire concept of Adam Smith implies. However, although the decisions affecting the bulk of the activity, as measured by money, are free of direct government control, the indirect restraint of government is definitely felt by the private segment. There are tariffs, which limit trade between nations and increase the cost of the articles that are still traded in spite of the barriers. There are minimum wage laws, pure food and drug acts which restrict production of certain goods; banking laws which restrict the opening of new banks and often set the interest rates which the bank can charge. The private segment helps support the public segment by donations, which are sometimes deductible in the computation of income taxes.

The commercial world deals with the purchase and sale of goods and services. The financial world furnishes the capital for the sale of goods, and the industrial world handles the manufacturing.

The Position Statement[1] for the commercial concern is simpler because of the lack of complexity in the "inventory" or items on hand. (See Chapter 2.)

The Income Statement of the commercial firm is simpler than that of a manufacturing concern because the firm buys and sells finished products. It does not use raw materials, so that the computation of income is less complex than that used by a factory. (See Chapter 3.)

Industrial firms, which manufacture items from raw materials, have more complicated financial statements, due to the existence of inventory of raw materials, goods in process, and, finally, finished goods. They use many different methods of determining the cost of goods manufactured and cost of goods still in process. The hardest problem in cost determination is that of allocating the fixed portion of the costs. This is related to the problem of capacity. If a plant designed to manufacture 100,000 units produces only 75,000 units, then the costs of the 25,000 *not* produced, or 25 percent of the total fixed costs, were the cost of *not* producing. This is in contrast to the methods which charge *all* fixed costs to production at the end of the year. It is valuable to be able to advise the management about the cost of what they did *not* produce. (See Chapter 5 on efficiency for an analysis of this problem.)

The financial institutions of the private segment of the economy deal primarily with money; that is, one firm loans money to others. The money they loan is borrowed from others at a lower rate of interest. Included are commercial banks, investment banks, savings banks, savings and loan associations, and insurance companies. The financial statements

---

[1]The "Position Statement" has been known as the "Balance Sheet" or "Financial Position Statement." Since books of account always "balance" if there are no bookkeeping errors, the term "Position Statement," showing the position of the entity at an instant of time, is both more accurate and elegant than "Balance Sheet."

of these firms are quite different from those of other commercial and industrial organizations. Most of these firms are regulated to an extent by the Federal Comptroller of the Currency (banks), Federal Home Loan Bank Board (savings and loan), or by banking examiners of each of the 50 states.

When a bank, savings and loan association, or insurance company grants a loan, it makes extensive use of accounting data. It asks the prospective buyer to prepare a financial statement, usually audited by professional accountants, to support the loan request. This loan request may be that of the local merchant for $1,000, or for $10,000,000 such as that sought by Texas Oil Company in 1967.

In the private segment the reporting function is often fulfilled by the preparation, by management, of reports to the owners. In larger firms, especially those listed on stock exchanges, the management usually reports four times a year—three times in an abbreviated or interim fashion and the fourth time, at fiscal year-end, in a more detailed fashion. The year-end statements include the report of the independent auditor, who states his opinion as to the fairness of the report.

HOW DOES THE "HALF PUBLIC-HALF PRIVATE" SEGMENT FUNCTION?

The accounting problem in the "half-public-half-private" industries, such as the regulated public utilities and the subsidized aircraft manufacturers, is more complicated than that of the private segment, as prices to be charged are set by government agencies. This means that more records must be prepared than in the cases of the private businesses. The public utilities (gas, transportation, electricity, telephone, and water) are subject to strict regulation by either Federal or state governments, or both. These government agencies prescribe the accounting system—even the account numbers in some states. They determine depreciation policies, which alter rates, and ultimately set the rate of return on the investment, which affects the price of the stock owned by the stockholders. As the Federal government has been in the field of producing and selling electricity since shortly after World War I at Muscle Shoals, the accounting records of private utilities have become vital to prove competitive costs relative to the Federal operation, which pays no income taxes and seldom contributes to local government costs.

The public utilities are also considered to be "regulated monopolies" in that two gas companies are not permitted to serve the same street. In return for this special treatment by government, resulting in lower costs, the rates should be lower.

The industries, which are subsidized by the government, usually the Federal government, reflect the subsidies as income. The determination of degree of profitableness is quite different when the "deficit" or "loss" is to be made up by the taxpayers.

Presumably there could be two categories—direct subsidies and contracts. At times in U.S. history there have been many direct subsidies, but now the contracts are probably more important. More than $60 billion per year is being spent on armaments, which is largely contract business. Some of these firms are paid merely to be *prepared* to manufacture, without any present real production, while others are manufacturing goods to be exploded.

HOW DOES THE PUBLIC SEGMENT FUNCTION?

Elected government officials are entitled to regular reports of the activities, measurable in terms of money, of those persons under their direction. Government accounting, as well as that of certain nonprofit organizations, is known as *fund accounting,* partly because there are no income or loss concepts in the same sense as in the private segment and because each "fund" is kept separate. The government is *not* designed to make money (although some governments have sufficient income from such items as oil royalty that they charge no sales, income, or property taxes), but it is supposed to prepare carefully and thoroughly a budget for the future and then assess the citizens enough to finance the budget by the use of one tax or another.

As all government business is *public* business, these periodic reports prepared for the governing bodies should also be available to private citizens. There is room for improvement in readability of government reports, especially in the treatment of long-term projects where a commitment is made for a large project that might take many years to finish. Each year only the cash outlay for that year is shown as an expenditure. But the obligation for the entire project has been incurred which would probably be useless if the work were stopped part way through. Another complexity is in the case of an appropriation which has not been entirely spent by the end of the fiscal (accounting) year. These unexpended amounts are not always clearly reflected in subsequent budgets and therefore offer opportunity for management manipulation.

The limitations of the one-year period used in reporting government activities could be overcome by preparing a Long-Term Budget, which would include the commitments to spend beyond the current year and also the appropriations of funds made for these commitments. As the assets were completed, they would be transferred from the Long-Term Budget to the Position Statement of the government agency.

Any unspent balances of current appropriations that could be legally carried over into the succeeding period can be shown on this Long-Term Budget.

These complications are found most often in the Federal government, where there is an added reporting problem, because the Federal government is the only agency that can "issue" money. The Treasury can increase the national debt by issuing U.S. Government securities, or by changing the requirements for the bank reserve ratios and interest rates, via another arm of the government known as the Federal Reserve Bank. Thus the economy and, ultimately, the financial status of the central government can be effectively changed.

Local Government

Most local-government budgets and reports are prepared by funds, i.e., the general fund, the sewer fund, or the park fund. Each of these funds has assets, including cash, and can also have debts including bonds, which are sold to investors in order to finance the project concerned. Some local governments operate enterprises which are similar to private enterprise, and if they yield a net income at the end of the year they then increase the revenue of one of the funds of the government. Refuse collection, for which a fee is charged, may result in net income.

International agencies, including the United Nations and its related agencies, also handle funds. These agencies report to the respective member countries, who in turn sometimes report to their own citizens.

One wonders what type of government report will be needed for the interplanetary organization.

WHAT SUPPORTS THE PUBLIC SEGMENT?

The cost of government operations is financed from many sources including taxes, borrowing, licenses, fines, and also receipts earmarked for so-called "trust funds" such as the Federal social-security trust fund. The various types of taxes assessed and collected are discussed in Chapter 11.

HOW DO THE DIFFERENCES IN LEGAL ORGANIZATION AFFECT ACCOUNTING?

An individual business may be owned by a sole proprietor or, in community property states, by husband and wife. Legally an individual proprietorship is not different from the individual himself. However, an accounting of the business unit involves making a distinction between the business and personal assets and liabilities.

In the case of the first three types, individual proprietors, partnerships, and joint ventures, there is a liability problem which is important in choosing the type of organization. The individual (whether one person or husband and wife jointly) is responsible for all of his debts, and there is no distinction between business and personal assets as far as the creditors are concerned. However, in certain states the residence, used as the home, can be "homesteaded," which in most cases prevents the loss of the home to creditors in the event of financial difficulties.

Partnership

The partnership, which is in reality an extension of the individual beyond the family unit, always has one general partner whose personal assets are available for the creditors if needed. The "limited" partners are limited in their loss to the amounts invested. The partnership is in some ways more flexible than the corporation in that there is usually only one group of people concerned, for the owners are often the managers. In a corporation there is a necessary specialization of function by stockholders, directors, officers, and employees.

Joint Venture

A particular type of partnership is the joint venture, which in effect is a partnership only for a particular operation—for example, a certified public accountant and an attorney may own an office building jointly. They have in effect a partnership only for the building, but not in their practices nor in any other sense.

Corporation

The corporation involves limited liability. In fact the abbreviation "Ltd" often appears after the name of a corporation. This type of legal organization is a creation of one of the states of the union, as each state is empowered to grant charters (after the filing of the articles of incorporation) to organizers to do business as a corporation. The Federal government and certain state governments, grant charters to cooperatives, frequently in agriculture, which are corporations that pay no income tax if the income is all distributed to the owners and customers. This is a definite advantage, as the commercial corporation pays Federal and state income taxes on earnings, and a penalty tax if certain earnings are not distributed. Besides these taxes each stockholder must include dividends received, in his income tax return each year, subject to a minor amount of exclusion on the Federal tax.

The commercial corporation has many advantages over the partnership and individual, in spite of the possible tax disadvantages mentioned above, in that the charter is usually perpetual, the shares can be willed by an owner, and the corporation is not dissolved upon the death of a stockholder. Secondly, as mentioned above, the limited liability is very significant to the investor. Third, his interest in a corporation is more easily sold than would be his interest in a partnership. Doing business in the form of corporations has played an important role in the growth of this nation's economy. It has permitted the pooling of individual resources for ventures which require large amounts of capital well beyond the means of sole proprietors or partnerships. Without the advantage of limited liability the growth of American corporations would have been difficult if not impossible.

Trusts and Estates

The categories of trusts and estates are included here because the trustee (of the trust) or executor (of the estate) is often required to operate a going concern for several years before he can distribute the assets. Some trusts continue for a generation until the assets are distributed to the second generation. The trust assets are usually invested in shares of a business rather than in an entire business, but in either event financial statements must be prepared for the trustee and the beneficiaries.

HOW DOES THE TAX-EXEMPT SEGMENT FUNCTION?

Most tax-exempt activities have been incorporated because the liability is limited to the assets of the corporation rather than to the assets of the members of an unincorporated association. The tax-exempt status can pertain both to the exemption from paying Federal and state income taxes, and to receiving tax-deductible donations from individuals or commercial corporations. In many states these organizations also receive exemptions from local property taxes. These exemptions are obtained by applying to the government agencies concerned and are allowed under statutory provisions of the governing body.

Even though the tax-exempt organizations do not have to pay income taxes, except on unrelated income, most of them are required to file tax returns each year and thus need to prepare financial statements for the tax returns. The financial statements and audit reports are also needed to fulfill the responsibility of management to the donors. These are usually prepared on a fund-accounting basis showing for each fund the opening balance, receipts, disbursements, and closing balance whether in cash or in other assets.

Each of the different groups uses slightly different record-keeping procedures. The private educational institutions, which derive part of their income from endowment investments and part from tuition fees, have developed procedures for calculating the cost for each student each year. Hospitals and rest homes develop costs per bed per day and also have systems to meet the unit cost requirements of Medicare, which reimburses, with Federal tax receipts, partial costs for certain patients.

Many foundations have been established in recent years. If their purposes are approved by the Federal and state governments, then their income is not taxable. Part or all of their grants to an individual may be tax-exempt to him.

Churches have need for accounting reports of specialized types. They and their related institutions are exempt from income and property taxes.

In many communities groups of individuals start activities, such as an art association, which might qualify for income tax exemption if proper application is made. If such exemption is not received, then the donation of the individual members is not deductible, and may be questioned or disallowed on members' income tax returns.

Chapter 2

How To Inventory and Record Economic Wealth

GENERAL CONCEPTS

The storing-up of "wealth" has gone on ever since man first made a spear to kill animals and then hid food in a cave for future use. In this simple case the spear, probably made of wood, was not burned as firewood but saved; likewise the food was not eaten immediately but stored or preserved for later consumption. Today the spear is called "equipment" and the food called "inventory." The equipment is classified, along with buildings or structures, as *long-life assets* and is subject to *depreciation*. Depreciation reflects the wearing out of an asset and is an expense for income tax purposes. As expenses are deductible from revenue, they reduce income. Also in the long-life group are depletable raw materials, which occur in nature and cannot be replaced by man (such as coal, iron ore); intangible assets are patents, franchises, and other rights which are amortized or written off for accounting purposes.

The inventory, in the modern world, consists basically of raw materials (not yet put into process of fabrication), goods in process, or those that are partly completed, and finished goods ready for sale. Other classifications will be considered later. Different methods of reporting wealth have been developed and are necessary to present information to enable management to make decisions.

A tabulation of national wealth appears in Table 2-1. The classifications, in the table, used by economists, are somewhat different from those used by accountants, but they can be somewhat reconciled. For example,

TABLE 2-1
National Wealth—Component Parts

Structures	Inventories
Nonfarm	Private
Nonresidential	Public
Government	Monetary gold and silver
Institutional	Land
Mining*	Public
Other*	Private
Residential	Net foreign assets
Farm*	
Equipment	
Producer durables*	
Consumer durables	

*NOTE: Subject to depreciation.
SOURCE: R. W. Goldsmith, *A Study of Saving in the United States,* Princeton University Press, 1956, as shown in the *Statistical Abstract of the United States* (1965), p. 351.

the reproducible tangible assets are called long-life assets by accountants. Some captions, such as net foreign assets, have no comparable accounting term. Estimated data for the items in Table 2-1 are given in the *Statistical Abstract of the United States.*

WEALTH VS. INCOME

Wealth is the value of things at an instant of time, whereas income is the sum of (a) the flow of receipts during a period of time and (b) the increase in value of the wealth or stock.

As specific time periods are needed for management and tax purposes, the year has been determined to be the most useful period. In the accounting world the Position Statement reflects the wealth at an instant of time, whether it be prepared for the private business organization, a governmental unit, or a tax-exempt foundation. The Income Statement, discussed in a later chapter, reflects certain of the changes in Position Statements at the beginning and the end of the year. The difference between the economists' definition of wealth and income[1] and the accountants' concept is that at present the accountant does *not* reflect increase in value due to price increases, called inflation, because basically the financial statements are prepared on an *historical* cost basis.

[1] "Personal income may be defined . . . as the result obtained by adding consumption during the period to 'wealth' at the end of the period and the subtracting 'wealth' at the beginning." Henry C. Simons, *Personal Income Taxation,* University of Chicago Press, Chicago, 1937, p. 50.

"INSTANT-OF-TIME CONCEPT" APPLIED

If the year is chosen for a particular income-reporting period, then a choice is necessary as to what is the beginning of the year. Under Federal income tax law the first of any month may be used. The Long-Term Budget, for more than one year is useful when projects are of longer duration. Both the budget, or plan for the future, and Income or Operations Statement of the results may be for this longer period. We also assume the principle of "continuity," that the firm will continue after the inventory is taken and values determined. One chooses an arbitrary point in time to make an evaluation. However, the business, government, or tax-exempt organization does not stop its operation while the accountants take inventory. Therefore, a complicated system of "cutoffs" is required in order to obtain the needed data. For example, business has to decide that all goods received after 4:00 p.m. on December 30 will be counted in the next year, especially if December 31 is a holiday. Government may have to decide that after some certain time all fines for traffic tickets will be recorded in the subsequent year. If these decisions are constant from year to year, the data will be comparable.

A sample Position Statement, typical of many in private business, is shown in Table 2-2 with assets, liabilities, and owner's equity. In order to understand the meaning of a Position Statement it is necessary to review some conventions or customs that are not evident in the statement itself. The asset section is arranged, insofar as possible, in order of "liquidity," or convertibility to cash. The first part in this section is the current assets, those which will be converted to cash within one year in the ordinary course of a going business. Within the current assets the cash items come first. This category includes cash in bank, cash on hand, "imprest" cash used for payment of small bills, and also for change in the cash register, and cash in transit perhaps from branches of the firm. Securities of the central government would come next, then other readily salable short-term investments. Amounts owed to the firm are represented by accounts and notes receivable due within a year from the date of the statement. The accounts receivable are usually due within 30 days, unless they are installment accounts which are shown differently in the statement. If the firm is on the allowance basis, for income tax purposes, then the allowance for doubtful accounts, known as a *valuation account*, comes next.

Inventory would follow and it might be only the inventory of finished goods, as in a retail store, or it might consist of three main categories if the firm were a manufacturer—namely, raw materials, goods in process, and finished goods.

TABLE 2-2

Position Statement — Private Segment

(As at December 31, 196X)

100 Assets (things owned)

110 Current Assets:
    111   Cash in bank . . . . $ 9,500
    112   Cash on hand.   100
    113   U.S. Government securities.   10,000
    114   Accounts and notes receivable $25,000
    114A Less: Allowance for
           doubtful accounts
           and notes   1,200   23,800

    117   Inventory (basis to be noted).   20,000
    119   Prepaid expenses 3,000 $66,400

120 Investments
    121   Investment in subsidiary   13,000

130 Long-Life Assets — Tangible (at cost)
    131   Machinery. 20,000
    132   Buildings 50,000
                           70,000
    131–132A Less: Allowance for
                depreciation. 18,000   52,000
    135   Land   30,000   82,000

140 Long–Life Assets–Intangible (at cost)
    141   Organization expense   3,000
    141A Less: Allowance for
               amortization. 1,800   1,200
    147   Goodwill   10,000   11,200

150 Other Assets:
    151   Deposits   400

Total Assets $173,000

The second section of the statement contains the tangible long-life assets, sometimes called "fixed assets," but as most of these assets are depreciable or subject to wear, the adjective long-life seems more descriptive. (See Chapter 4 for discussion of detailed asset-valuation problems.)

    There are always intangible assets, including the portion of notes receivable due in a period longer than one year, investment in a subsidiary

TABLE 2-2 (*continued*)
Position Statement—Private Segment
(As at December 31, 196X)

200 Liabilities (debts)

210 Current Liabilities
    211 Accounts payable . . . . $ 7,000
    212 Accrued liabilities   2,000
    213 Notes payable   6,000
    214 Current portion of trust deed or
         mortgage payable—alternate
         for individuals. . . . .
    215 Current portion of bonds
         payable.   10,000
    216 Taxes, other than income taxes   1,200
    217 Income taxes payable (Federal
         and state)   1,400

                                    $ 27,600

220 Long-Term Liabilities*
    221 Trust deed or mortgage payable
         less: Current portion—alternate
         for individuals
    222 Bonds payable   100,000
         Less: current portion   10,000

                                      90,000

  Total Liabilities $117,600

300 Owner's Equity (net worth)
    (varies with type of ownership—see
    Table 2-3 for variations)   55,400

  Total Liabilities and Owner's Equity $173,000

*The individual proprietor and the partnership would not have the bonds payable, but the corporation could have both the bonds and the trust deed or mortgage. The trust deed and accompanying note payable are used in several states instead of the mortgage.

(usually a corporation owned for purposes of control), organization expense, and goodwill.

    The liabilities section of the statement differs from the asset section in that there are no valuation accounts, such as allowance for doubtful accounts or allowance for depreciation. Current liabilities are shown first, and are defined as those debts due to be paid within a year. The accounts payable are usually due within 30 days or sometimes within 10 days, if a

TABLE 2-3
Position Statement—Private Segment
Net Worth Sections Only
(As at December 31, 196X)

I.　Individual Proprietorship

Owner's Equity

Investment			$38,500
Personal 1/1/6X	$16,000		
Add: Income 196X	5,400		
	21,400		
Less: Drawing—Cash	$ 3,100		
Income taxes	1,400	4,500	16,900
Balance, 12/31/6X			$55,400

II.　Partnership—Messrs. A and B

	A	B	Total
Investment			
1/1/6X	$18,500	$10,000	$28,500
New investment 7/1/6X.		10,000	10,000
	18,500	20,000	38,500
Personal			
1/1/6X	10,000	6,000	16,000
Income: 6% on investment . . .	1,110	900	2,010
For time spent.	1,200	600	1,800
Balance equal to A and B . .	795	795	1,590
	3,105	2,295	5,400
Less: Drawing—cash	2,000	1,100	3,100
Income taxes	900	500	1,400
	2,900	1,600	4,500
	405	495	900
Personal 12/316X	10,405	6,495	16,900
Owner's Equity 12/31/6X	$28,905	$26,495	$55,400

paid before the end of the year. The income shown, as an increase to retained income (or earnings), is after taxes. The amount of Federal and state taxes was deducted in the Income Statement (Table 3-1.)

TABLE 2-3 (*continued*)
Position Statement—Private Segment
Net Worth Sections Only (*continued*)
(As at December 31, 196X)

III. Corporation—Owner's Equity*

1. Stock—Investment

Preferred stock, $100 par, $6 dividend, cumulative, nonparticipating, 10,000 shares authorized. 100 shares issued and outstanding.	$10,000
Capital in excess of par (preferred)	1,000
Common stock, no par, stated value $5, 100,000 shares authorized, 5,000 issued and outstanding.	25,000
Capital in excess of stated value (common).	2,500
Subtotal stock	38,500

2. Retained income (earnings)

1/1/6X.		$16,000	
Add: Income for 196X		4,000	
		20,000	
Less: Dividends			
Preferred	$ 600		
Common	2,500	3,100	16,900
			$55,400

*Assuming only one stockholder. Use term *owners'* if more than one stockholder.

POSITION STATEMENT—GOVERNMENT

Government accounting is known as "fund accounting," because of legal restrictions on the use of certain assets and the legal obligations represented by specific liabilities. As the accounting and reporting procedures for government at each of the various levels of city, township, county, state, and nation are much the same, a city will be used as an example (see Table 2-4). An Income Statement, usually called "Receipts and Disbursements," for each of the funds shown in Table 3-3. The data on the Position Statement and the Income Statement are combined in the Source and Application of Funds, in the chapter on special reports. The example contains the total of all funds and detail for each of the following funds:

1. General Fund
2. Special Assessment Fund
3. Trust Fund
4. Property Fund
   Bond Funds
5. Sinking Fund
6. Debt Fund

Some of the terminology in government accounting is different from that used in business accounting, so several explanations are needed in order to understand Table 2-4.

Taxes Receivable

Because much of the revenue of the General Fund is obtained from property taxes paid usually only twice a year and also because some tax-payers are always delinquent, there are amounts due to the fund at the end of the year or month.   As the receivables are collected over a period of years, the debt is paid and eventually this set of accounts disappears.

The other tangible long-life assets are the equipment, buildings, and land used by the city. These are also shown in the Property Fund. The intangible long-life assets consist, in this example, of two items: (1) *special assessments receivable*, which are amounts due to the Special-Assessment Fund from the owners of property in a specified area for improvements such as streets, sidewalks, or sewers, and (2) an *offset account* for the Debt Fund. In municipal accounting an offset is shown in this manner because the debts are not secured by specific assets, pledged like those which secure a mortgage or trust deed in the private segment. Because the tax-payers of the entire city are responsible for paying back liabilities, the debts and property are shown in separate funds.

Liabilities

There are two accounts in Table 2-4 that are unusual. One is the "contracts payable—retained percentage." This consists of amounts due contractors who have uncompleted contracts with the city. The amount due will be paid upon completion of the work. Deposits made to guarantee performance are treated in a similar manner.

The other unusual item is "interest payable in future years." This procedure of computing and recording interest payable in the future is unique in government accounting, as it is not used in the private segment. In this example the "future interest" is calculated to be $38,000 and the bonds payable in the Debt Fund amount to $100,000, or a total due of $138,000. This amount is shown in long-life assets—intangible as an offset account known as "amounts available and to be provided for retirement of bonds and interest"—a long title but quite descriptive!

Reserves

The "encumbrances" are important in government accounting. The amounts of encumbrances on the Position Statement are those determined to be expended, in the previous period, but not yet legally obligated as accounts payable. The "appropriations—unencumbered balance" is the balance of the previous year's business appropriated in the budget but not yet encumbered. For example, Table 2-4 shows "Encumbrances" of $57,450, of which $50,000 is in the General Fund and $7,450 in the Special Assessment Fund. When the purchasing procedures have been completed the encumbrances will move up into accounts payable in the current liabilities section of the Position Statement.

Fund Balances

This section is similar to the net-worth section of the Position Statement in the private segment. The "unappropriated surplus" is the term used for the net worth of the General Fund. The ownership of the Trust Fund assets is allocated into trust—principal and trust—income. The amount in the principal account represents the total that should be invested. Reference to the assets shows that of the $58,000 principal, $55,000 is in investments; therefore $3,000 of the $4,000 cash in bank belongs to the principal and is available for investment. The $1,000 income cash can be spent in accordance with the trust instrument. The latter may state that this amount is for a specific purpose, such as special material for the Recreation Department, perhaps in honor of a prominent civic leader. The last item is the property which represents the net worth of the Property Fund, or the physical assets of the city. In most cases no depreciation expense or allowance is shown in municipal or government accounts. This is unwise and short-sighted because many assets are really declining in economic usefulness yet if not depreciated they are shown at original cost.

TABLE 2-4

Cityville, U.S.A. Position Statement of All Funds (Detail of Each Fund as at June 30, 196X)

Assets	Total	General Fund	Special Assessment Fund	Trust Funds	Property Fund	Bonds	
						Sinking Fund	Debt Fund
Current Assets							
Cash in bank	$171,000	$139,500	$ 27,000	$ 4,000		$ 500	
Cash on hand	500	500					
Taxes receivable	40,000	40,000					
Interest receivable	550		500			50	
Materials and supplies	12,000	12,000					
	224,050	192,000	27,500	4,000		550	
Investments—at cost (market value $62,120)	64,800			55,000		9,800	
Long-Life Assets—Tangible							
Equipment (at cost)	59,000				$ 59,000		
Buildings (at cost)	171,000				171,000		
Land (at cost)	20,000				20,000		
	250,000				250,000		
Long-Life Assets—Intangible							
Special assessments receivable	90,000		90,000				
Amounts available and to be provided for retirement of bonds and interest	138,000						$138,000
	228,000		90,000				138,000
Total Assets	$766,850	$192,000	$117,500	$59,000	$250,000	$10,350	$138,000

Liabilities

Current Liabilities							
Accounts payable	$100,000	$ 95,000	$ 5,000				
Interest payable	400		400				
Contracts payable—retained percentage	8,500		8,500				
	108,900	95,000	13,900				
Long-Term Liabilities							
Bonds payable	191,000		91,000				$100,000
Interest payable in future years	38,000						38,000
	229,000		91,000				138,000
Reserves							
Encumbrances	57,450	50,000	7,450				
Retirement of sinking-fund bonds	10,400					$ 10,400	
Appropriations—unencumbered balance	5,000		5,000				
	72,850	50,000	12,450			10,400	
Fund Balances							
Unappropriated surplus (deficit)	46,950	47,000				(50)	
Unappropriated surplus interest	150		150				
Trust—principal	58,000			$ 58,000			
Income	1,000			1,000			
Property	250,000				$250,000		
	356,100	47,000	150	59,000	250,000	(50)	
Total	$766,850	$192,000	$117,500	$ 59,000	$250,000	$ 10,350	$138,000

TABLE 2-5
St. Swithin's-in-the-Field Church
Cityville, Pennsylvania
Position Statement
(As at December 31, 196X)

Assets	Total	General Purposes	Special Local Purposes†	Special Outside Purposes
Current Assets*				
Cash in checking account . . .	$ 1,700	$ 700	$ 400	$600
Investment-saving account. . .	10,000		10,000	
-savings and loan. .	5,000		5,000	
Pledges receivable (past due). .	2,000	2,000		
	18,700	2,700	15,400	$600
Long-Life Assets				
Land	30,000	30,000		
Buildings	150,000	150,000		
Equipment	20,000	20,000		
	200,000	200,000		
Total Assets	$218,700	$202,700	$15,400	$600
Liabilities				
Current Liabilities*				
Accounts payable	$ 900	$ 900	$	$
Loans payable (past due) . . .				
Payroll taxes	100	100		
Special offerings	600			600
	1,600	1,000		600
Loans Payable	80,000	80,000		
Total Liabilities.	$ 81,600	$ 81,000		$600
Net Worth—unappropriated . . .	135,100	119.700	15,400	
—Appropriated as reserve for pledges receivable	2,000	2,000		
	137,100	121,700	15,400	
Total Liabilities and Net Worth	$218,700	$202,700	$15,400	$600

*"Current assets" have a specialized meaning. There is no account comparable to accounts receivable resulting from sales in the business segment. Likewise "current liabilities" include only the past-due portion of loans payable, if any, rather than the portion of the debt due in the next twelve months, which is done in the business segment.

†Funds for Special Local Purposes could include a Building Fund, an Organ Fund, or funds for specific other purposes. A subsidiary ledger is to be maintained for each fund.

POSITION STATEMENT—CHURCH

The "Position Statement" for "St. Swithin's in-the-Field Church" is shown in Table 2-5. The procedures behind the preparation of this statement and of the Revenue and Expenses Statement shown in Table 3-4 are quite different from both the private segment and the government segment.

The church is used as an example of all tax-exempt or nonprofit organizations to which people voluntarily give money. In all cases the organization is required to obtain tax-exempt status from both Federal and state governments in order that the donations of the individuals be tax-exempt. The "nonprofitability" refers to the fact that any income from "unrelated enterprises" would become taxable. For example, a church may be requested to rent its parking lot on weekdays, which income would be unrelated to religious activity.

The Church Statement has three sets of funds:

1. General Purposes
2. Special Local Purposes
3. Special Outside Purposes

The General Purposes or general fund is controlled by the budget adopted by the governing group. This Position Statement is prepared by including only past due pledges receivable, which is not comparable to accounts receivable in the private segment. Also in the net-worth section there is an offsetting accounts for pledges receivable. In the liabilities section only past-due amount for loans payable would be included, whereas in the private segment the debt due during the next 12-months portion would be included.

Chapter 3

How To Classify Income

As this book is mainly concerned with financial affairs, it is not primarily focused on "esthetic" values, such as those associated with a beautiful sunset or work of art. The income we are concerned with here is income that is quantitatively measurable.

In the private segment the income is the increase in net worth between time periods for which Position Statements are prepared. (See Table 3-1.) If distributions have been made to owners—drawings or dividends—then these must be added back to the increase shown between the two Position Statements for a complete picture.

In fund accounting, used by the government and tax-exempt segments, the concept of income varies with each of several categories. The data in Tables 3-3 and 3-4 show these income concepts numerically.

HOW DOES INDIVIDUAL INCOME RELATE TO NATIONWIDE INCOME?

The incomes of the various segments make up the Nationwide Income (Table 3-2). Accountants have assisted in determining the income of each of the segments reporting to the Federal government, which then publishes the results of its tabulations. Nationwide Income is published in the following main categories:

Gross National Product (GNP)

Net National Product (NNP)

National Income (NI)

It is of interest in this book that the totals are part of the end product of the accounting process. More significant is the fact that management must take into account an estimated future Nationwide Income, or parts of it, in making decisions. These decisions for individual businesses ultimately affect the national economy.

In the private segment, decisions as to plant expansion may be based upon estimated future sales of a particular commodity. This estimate, in turn, probably was made at least in part on the basis of estimates of Nationwide Income.

In the private segment the final net income (gross income less taxes) is either retained in the business enterprise or it is distributed to the owners. These items are part of the Nationwide Income, but so also are wage payments, rent payments, and interest payments. Table 3-2 presents the relationship between the income of the various segments except that the income of the tax-exempt segment of the economy is not segregated by the statisticians who gather nationwide income data for many countries. Therefore, it is not shown separately here. The income of the tax-exempts would be mostly in the form of rent, interest, and dividends and

TABLE 3-1

Income Statement—Private Segment

(For year ended December 31, 196X)

410	Gross Sales		$104,000	
401R	Less: Sales returns and allowances		4,000	
	Net Sales...............................		100,000	100.0%
	Cost of Sales			
	120 Inventory 1/1/6X	$18,000		
	510 Purchases..................	60,000		
	520 Freight–in	2,000		
	Available	80,000		
	120 Less: Inventory 12/31/6X	20,000	60,000	60.0%
	Gross Operating Income		40,000	40.0%
600	Operating Expenses			
	601 Payroll	18,000		
	602 Payroll taxes	1,260		
	603 Group insurance	340		
	604 Repairs	370		
	605 Freight–out................	630		
	606 Travel	520		
	607 Licenses, dues, and subscriptions .	210		
	608 Rent	2,400		
	609 Utilities	320		
	610 Taxes–local................	1,500		
	612 Insurance–general	405		
	613 Workmen's compensation	220		
	614 Depreciation*	3,975		
	615 Amortization	300		
	Total operating expenses.................		30,450	30.4%

TABLE 3-1 (*continued*)
Income Statement—Private Segment

Net Operating Income			$ 9,550	9.6%
700	Other Expenses			
	701 Interest†	$ 4,500		
	702 Discounts given	200		
	703 Loss on sale of long-life assets ...	—		
	704 Doubtful accounts	150		
	705 Employees pension-plan costs ...	—	4,850	
			4,700	
800	Other Income			
	801 Interest	400		
	802 Discounts earned	300		
	803 Gain on sale of long-life assets ...	—	700	
Net Income Before Income Taxes			5,400	5.4%
	710 Less: State income tax‡....................		270	
Net Income Before Federal Income Tax			5,130	
	720 Less: Federal income tax‡.................		1,130	
Net Income to Retained Income			$ 4,000	4.0%

*New machinery of $2,000 and new buildings $20,000 completed October 1, machinery on a depreciation basis of 10 years and buildings 20 years.
†An additional $50,000 borrowed July 1.
‡5 Percent state income tax and 22 percent Federal income tax.

TABLE 3-2
Nationwide Income—Component Parts

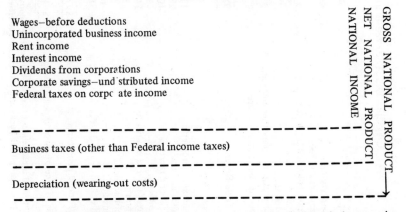

Wages—before deductions
Unincorporated business income
Rent income
Interest income
Dividends from corporations
Corporate savings—undistributed income
Federal taxes on corporate income

Business taxes (other than Federal income taxes)

Depreciation (wearing-out costs)

ASSUMPTIONS: A closed economy, i.e., no foreign trade and also no price changes during the period.

TABLE 3-3

Cityville, U.S.A. Revenue and Expenditures Statement (For the year ended 6/30/196X)

| | | | Special | | | Bonds | |
| | | | Assessment | Trust | Property | Sinking | Debt |
Revenue	Total	General Fund	Fund	Fund	Fund	Fund	Fund
Property taxes	$620,000	$620,000					
Licenses and fees	50,000	50,000					
Taxes collected by state*	250,000	250,000					
Fines	35,000	35,000					
Interest	3,550			$ 3,000		$ 550	
Subventions from other governments	30,000	30,000					
Special assessments—interest	150		$ 150				
Total Receipts	988,700	985,000	150	3,000		550	
Expenditures							
General government	170,000	170,000					
Police and fire	280,000	280,000					
Parks and recreation†	103,000	100,000		3,000			
Sanitation	90,000	90,000					
Streets and storm drains	160,000	160,000					
Library	30,000	30,000					
Debt service	70,600	70,600					
Pensions	60,000	60,000				600	
Other	10,000	10,000					
Total expenditures	$973,600	$970,000		$ 3,000		$ 600	
Excess of receipts over expenditures	$ 15,100	$ 15,000	$ 150	$ 0		$ (50)	

*Could include sales tax, motor vehicle licenses, and gasoline taxes.
†Assuming that parks and recreation activities are the beneficiaries of the income of the trust funds.

therefore is included along with the rent, interest, and dividends received by others in the economy.

Municipal Revenue and Expenditures

In contrast to the Income Statement of the private segment, which shows net income after taxes, for the results of the production of goods or services, is the Revenue and Expenditures Statement of a municipality (Table 3-3). This statement shows the changes during a year and the financial condition of the City at the end of the year is shown in Table 2-4, Position Statement of All Funds, Cityville, U.S.A.

Similar statements could be prepared for the other units of government including counties, townships, and even the Federal government.

Table 3-3 has been prepared on the accrual basis—not on the cash basis, as usual in governmental accounting. This is clearly shown by studying the Position Statement (Table 2-4) where accrued assets of taxes receivable and accrued liabilities of several kinds are shown. This approach to governmental accounting would present to the governing bodies and to those electing them a clearer understanding of the financial situation.

Church Revenue and Expenses

The church operating statement, showing Revenue and Expenses, (Table 3-4) has several differences from the statement for the private segment yet both reflect the results of transactions.

As most churches take up collections at the services, the term "loose plate" is used for the cash which is unidentified as to donor. The identified cash or checks is known as "pledges" or special donations. Churches often have endowment investments which yield interest or dividend income. These revenue items are classified in three main categories: (1) general purposes, (2) special local purposes, and (3) special outside purposes. The general purposes are subject to budgetary control. The special local purposes usually are restricted by the donor and thus kept separate. The donation itself may be restricted as to use or it may be invested and the income, only, used for a restricted purpose. The building fund, which later increases long-life assets, may be one of these funds. The third group, the special outside purposes, consists of collections for purposes outside of the local church unit. For example, when a fund drive is put on to raise money for a specific activity such as a children's home or a home for the aged, then the funds are all transferred to the specific beneficiary and the balance is zero. If funds are left at the end of the accounting period, they show as a liability.

TABLE 3-4
St. Swithins-in-the-Field-Church
Cityville, U.S.A.
Revenue and Expenses (For the Year Ended December 31, 196X)

	Total	General Purposes	Special Local Purposes	Special Outside Purposes
Revenue				
Loose-plate collections...............	$ 8,000	$ 8,000	$	$
Pledges............................	84,000	82,000		2,000
Special donations...................	8,000	4,000	3,000	1,000
Interest or dividends.................	600		600	
Other..............................	200	200		
	100,800	94,200	3,600	3,000

Expenses				
Special offerings..........	2,400	2,400			2,400
Missionary Share	47,000	47,000		
Clergy—salaries	20,000	20,000		
rent	3,600	3,600		
utilities	700	700		
pension	3,000	3,000		
car	1,800	1,800		
Lay workers—salaries	8,000	8,000		
pension	1,200	1,200		
car	600	600		
Social-security taxes	300	300		
Church—utilities	2,000	2,000		
interest	2,400	2,400		
repairs	600	600		
Insurance	200	200		
Taxes	500	500	200	
Supplies	800	600	400	
Other	1,600	1,200	600	
	47,300	$ 46,700	$ 600	
	96,700	93,700	600	2,400
Excess of revenue over expenses...........	$ 4,100	$ 500	$ 3,000	$ 600
Other Receipts & Expenditures				
Loan from bank...........	$ 80,000	$ 80,000		
Cost of building...........	(80,000)	(80,000)		
	-0-	-0-		

HOW DOES INCOME, ON A CURRENT-PRICE BASIS, RELATE TO AN HISTORICAL-COST BASIS?

In a period of inflation the book values of assets are shown at less than current market value as the depreciable assets are stated at historical cost, less depreciation, and land at historical cost. Inventories are often less than current cost, due to the pricing method permitted by the taxing authorities which is discussed in a later chapter. Accounts receivable, due from customers, are shown less an allowance for doubtful accounts. This net figure may be less than actual collections. These practices reflect the so-called principle of *conservatism* since the assets are understated while the liabilities are tabulated at the actual amounts due. However, this conservatism in the asset account may lead to rank *radicalism* in the income accounts because, for example, low-asset values lead to low deductions for depreciation—which yields higher estimates of income!

As long as the principle of conservatism is followed as an appropriate practice, income will not be on a current-price basis. It is still the recommendation of the profession and the regulatory bodies that historical cost be continued to avoid arbitrary evaluations. The related Position Statements are also prepared on this conservative basis, so that the Income Statements are *consistent.* In the periods of rising prices, if depreciation is limited to historical cost, it is evident that the depreciation allowances made on the Position Statement are not sufficient for replacement of the assets. The income of past periods is therefore overstated and the income tax overpaid.

Other possible variations from a precise historical-cost basis will be considered in the chapter on valuations. If the current-price concept is important, then a supplementary set of Position and Income Statements can be made. Assets can then be shown on an estimated current basis and income adjusted likewise. One of the reasons that the current-price basis has not be used for financial statements is that business cycles have included both inflation and deflation. The current-price concept would mean a reduction of asset values during a period of deflation. Such major deflation has not happened for several years, but historically it occurred in 1907, 1921, and 1929-32.

Annual Income

As the year has become the time unit for most accounting reports, the problem of allocating costs to each of these years involves the valuations of the Position Statement. For example, if a machine is depreciated over a 10-year period rather than a 15-year period, both the income and income taxes are reduced while the cash available in the business is increased during the 10-year period and reduced in later periods, if the machine is still in use.

Another advantage of a yearly accounting period is that it is useful to be able to discuss *rates* of income per year. In this case the income is expressed as ratio to sales or ownership. Future rates of return on investment, perhaps for each of the next 10 years, also require the concept of annual income.

PART **II**

VALUES
AND
EFFICIENCY

Chapter **4**

How To Determine Present and Future Values: Significance for the Measurement of Income

Regardless of the type of organization, problems of the value of assets for the financial statements are common to all. If government agencies or tax-exempt organizations are planning to sell assets, they have a problem of evaluation. The completion of a transaction or exchange of assets—for example, cash for land—gives rise to new values for accounting purposes. Government and tax-exempt organizations may list currently owned assets at a possible market value, before they are sold, so as to be able to budget the future receipts from sales. In the private segment the valuation of assets is necessary for income tax purposes and is based on historical cost (amount actually paid, less depreciation), since appraisals or future values are not allowed by the taxing authorities.

Organizations invest funds in shares of other companies or in debt, such as a mortgage or bonds, which yield a fixed amount, if purchased at par or face value. If the investment is in shares, there is a problem of determining a price which should be paid when purchased. If the shares are listed on a stock exchange, then on most days there are enough willing buyers and sellers to establish a market for shares. If management thinks the price is too high, it must wait until a more propitious time to buy. If the purchaser contemplates buying all of the equity in a business corporation, there is probably no market in the sense of the stock market. Here the buyer and seller each figure out what they think the business is worth and bargain until an agreeable price is determined.

The price is based upon the estimated flow of income in the future, i.e., estimated earnings per year for an indefinite future period. If it is deemed to be low in risk, then the rate (called *discount*) used to arrive at present value is low. For example, if the estimated earnings of the small corporation were $20,000 per year and 5 percent was considered as a reasonable return, then the business would be worth 20 times $20,000 or $400,000. If it were considered to be quite risky and a 20 percent return was expected to cover such hazard, then the price would be 5 times $20,000 or $100,000. The general principle covering these cases is that annual return equals capital value times the interest rate. Therefore the value of an asset whose yield is expected to continue indefinitely equals the amount of the yield divided by the interest rate.

PARTS OF THE BUSINESS ORGANIZATION

In the above example the future needed to be considered as the value of a business was being estimated. When a value is put on the assets of a going concern, accountants are basically conservative. The future values are *not* reflected even in a period of inflation (devaluation of the dollar), nor are present values reflected as financial statements are on an original-cost-less-depreciation (wearing out) basis. It has been suggested that appraised, or current market value, should be shown on financial statements. This raises the question as to who should make the appraisal and how often should it be done. In the case of a request for a loan, the bank officer often desires to make his own inspection and appraisal before granting the loan.

Two major categories of assets will be considered for evaluation procedures. First, those that are tangible—i.e., physical assets—and second, the intangible, or rights to value.

Tangible Assets

The bases are as follows:

Investments

Short-term industrial bonds and U.S. government bonds shown at cost with market value in parentheses.

Receivables

Accounts and notes, both shown reduced by some figure for estimated reduction in value, due to "bad debts."

Inventory

Several methods of pricing the inventory, of goods held for sale, are available. The main methods in use are Last In First Out (LIFO), Average, and First In First Out (FIFO). Three less frequently used methods are Base Stock, NIFO (Next In First Out or replacement value), HIFO (Highest In First Out), which are not permitted for income tax calculations. Many companies have adopted the LIFO method, since it was first permitted by the Federal tax authorities and subsequently by many states. This is usually a change from FIFO, which assumes that the earliest purchases are sold first. Of course, this is the way goods are handled physically, as the "old cabbages" are sold first. The effect of LIFO is to offset the inflation. This method assumes that the earliest goods purchased, perhaps five years ago, at lower prices, are still on hand when in reality they have been sold. This system has the effect of reducing income and income taxes below

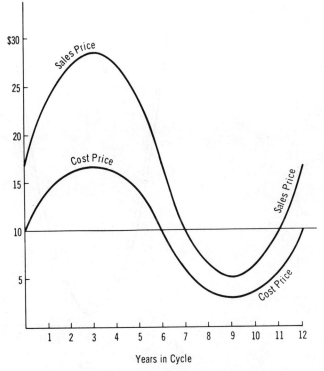

FIG. 4-1.   Business-cycle pattern for LIFO-FIFO contrast
(based on figures in Appendix Table A-2).

what they would have been under FIFO during a period of rising prices. However, during an entire long-term business cycle all methods yield the same results. The income tax return is for a period of one year. Thus the decision as to method of inventory valuation to be used must be based on this short period of time rather than on an entire cycle. (See Fig. 4-1.)

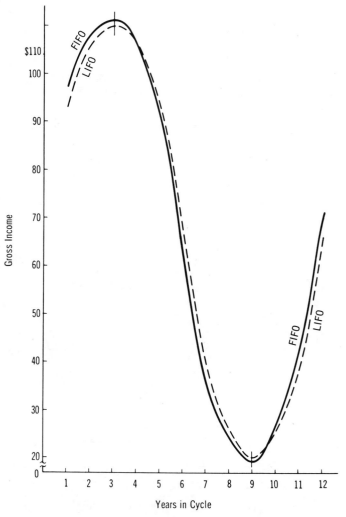

FIG. 4-2. LIFO results on income during cycle (based on data in Appendix Table A-2).

During the period when prices are above average (boom times), the net taxable income is less than under FIFO. In the second part of the diagrammatic business cycle (depression period), the losses are less under LIFO. Figure 4-1 shows the cost price of an article above and below the average of $10 over a 12-year cycle. Since business cycles are not as regular in real life as the one diagrammed, it may be difficult to realize the consequences of all points of the cycle. In Figs. 4-1, 4-2, and 4-3 it assumed that there are four three-year periods, namely—expansion, contraction, depression,

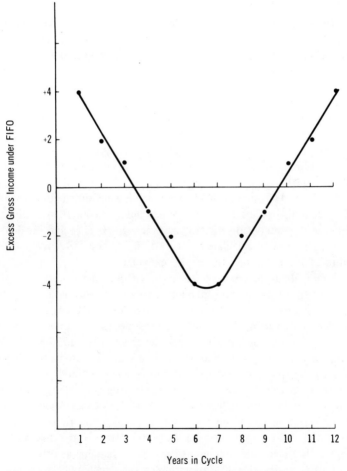

FIG. 4-3. LIFO vs. FIFO inventory variations in gross income under FIFO and LIFO (based on data in Appendix Table A-2).

and recovery. The result of LIFO on gross income (sales less costs) is shown in Fig. 4-2. During the first three years FIFO results in higher profits. During the next six-year decline, profits under LIFO are greater. During the last three years of recovery, FIFO yields higher profits. Most of the recent years have been in the expansion part of the cycle, as prices have increased quite steadily with only a few minor setbacks. Figure 4-2 demonstrates the variations above and below average during the 12-year period.

Machinery and Buildings

These man-made assets are said to be "depreciable," i.e., the value on the Position Statement is reduced by an account called allowance for depreciation and the gross income is reduced by depreciation expense. As the increases in the allowance and in the expense are equal, the effect of depreciation is twofold and both parts are of equal significance. The revaluation of the asset, due to wearing out, is reflected on the Position Statement. This revaluation reduces total assets. The usefulness to production is shown on the Income Statement as an expense.

The three most common methods of computing depreciation are (1) straight-line, or equal amounts per unit of time or of product, (2) declining-balance, or an equal percentage on the remaining balance per unit of time, and (3) sum-of-the-digits, which is a simplified approximation of the declining-balance method. For example, when a 10-year life is assumed, then the sum of the digits 1, 2, 3 through 10, is 55 and the depreciation the first year is calculated to be 10/55 or about 18 percent as compared to 10 percent in the straight-line example.

The Federal government has been encouraging investments, since 1958, by permitting an extra 20 percent first-year depreciation on "tangible personal property" to the extent of $10,000 of the cost. Since 1962 the Federal government has allowed an investment tax credit of as much as 7 percent of assets purchased during the year. Since 1954 the Federal government has also permitted rapid depreciation, based on either the sum-of-the-digits or "percentage of declining balance" method. State governments have followed on some of these programs. Many economists believe that reductions in income tax encourage increased investment so that the resulting rise in employment of persons will thus increase the Gross National Product. Figure 4-4 shows the effect of the three methods of depreciation. The lines represent the value remaining as residual at the end of each year. Thus the assets under the declining-balance and the sum-of-the-digits methods decrease much faster, during the first few years, than they would under the straight-line method.

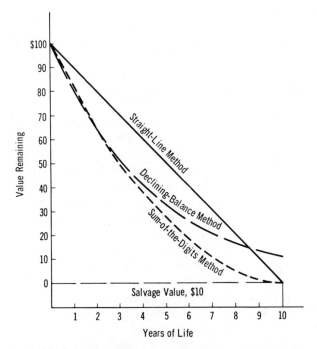

FIG. 4-4. Depreciation methods comparison of remaining balances, 10-year period (based on data in Appendix Table A-3).

Land

Land is not depreciable, nor are certain charges, such as street assessments, which must be added to the value of the land rather than taken as expenses.

Natural Resources

The natural resources, such as coal, oil, minerals, or lumber, which are nonreproducible by man, are said to be depleted as used. A depletion expense, computed as a percentage of revenue, is permitted to be deducted in computing taxable income. In this case the procedure is in contrast to the depreciation of machinery in that depletion expense can be deducted to compute taxable income as long as the resource is being taken from the earth, regardless of original cost. In the case of machinery and buildings, or man-made items, the expense deduction stops when book value (cost less depreciation) is reduced to salvage value.

Intangible Assets

These assets, or rights, are often worth much more than the cost shown on the Position Statements, but the accountants are conservative and thus do not reflect such market value. These rights may include trademark names or advertising symbols already established as identification for products.

Patents and copyrights are valued at the development cost, which can either be capitalized at the time it is incurred or written off. If the latter system is used, then the asset value is even less than cost. As patents are good for 17 years and copyrights for 28 years, those periods or shorter ones are used for amortization of the costs.

Franchises are the exclusive right to do business in a particular community or the exclusive right to sell a particular commodity. These are valued at cost and written off over the life of the right. A leasehold is the payment for the right to sublease property and is written off over the life of the lease. An "agreement not to compete" protects the buyer of a business from competition by the seller opening a second similar business. Its cost can be written off over the life of the agreement.

One item that is often misunderstood is "goodwill," partly because accountants record only the cost of goodwill, or the difference between the price paid for assets and the "fair market" value at the date of purchase. All well-known products are said to generate "goodwill" or reputation for satisfaction for the owners, but this is not recorded on the Position Statement. The recorded goodwill cannot be amortized or written off for income tax purposes.

Chapter **5**

How May Efficiency Be Achieved?

The Income and Position Statements, discussed in previous chapters, do not show alternative situations, but results. How these results come about involves a study of efficiency which is said to be the capacity to produce desired results. The study of efficiency is presented primarily in the private segment and particularly for the manufacture of goods, either durable or for consumption. Before outlays for long-life assets are made, decisions are still possible as to the type of long-life asset to be purchased. Once this decision has been made, the long-life assets are said to be "fixed," and the concern is said to be operating in the "short run" in the economic sense. Included in this fixed category are land, buildings, and machinery. The cost of using these long-life assets is called Fixed Costs. They include depreciation, or rent if property is not owned, property taxes, fire insurance, and standby costs of utilities. Certain central office and administrative costs are also fixed.

The other category of costs is called Variable Costs, because they change with changes in output. Included are labor, payroll taxes and fringe benefits, raw materials and purchased parts, and other costs which increase with increased production or decrease when output slows down.

In the private segment the desired result is to maximize the income or profit, by the use of assets available to the management. In the government segment and the tax-exempt segment the results are usually expressed in terms of services rendered to certain groups of people. The principle of efficiency is also useful in this segment, but the *results* are harder to measure.

The total economic activity in the community, including all three segments, measured in part by the Gross National Product, discussed in an earlier chapter, and in part by services not reducible to dollar values, is optimized when efficient use is made of all components.

EFFICIENCY IN THE PRIVATE SEGMENT

In the private segment the theoretical pattern of efficiency for a firm can be expressed in diagrammatic form such as shown in Fig. 5-1. The input items, or factors, are grouped into two parts, namely "variable"

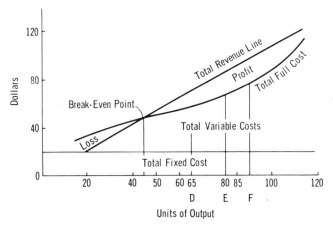

FIG. 5-1. Cost curves—totals.

factors, such as labor and meterials, and "fixed" factors such as land, buildings, and machinery. Figures 5-1 and 5-2 deal with the short run—that is, a period in which the amount of the fixed assets are assumed to be constant, and thus the variable expenses include the cost of labor, the cost of raw material used to make the product, and the variable portion of what is called overhead. (The unchanging portion of the overhead is the fixed cost.) An example of the variable cost of overhead is the cost of any electricity which is greater than the minimum standby charge. The standby charge is a fixed cost and the cost which exceeds this standby charge, will vary with the use of machines. If they are operated, in one week, more hours than in the previous week, then the variable cost for electricity is said to have increased.

The second major assumption in Figs. 5-1 and 5-2 is that the price, at which the article is sold, is constant or fixed as far as the producer is concerned. This is an example of "perfect competition" and therefore the total revenue line in Fig. 5-1 is a straight line and not a curve as would be the case in imperfect, or monopolistic, competition. The price line, or average revenue, is a horizontal straight line which denotes that the producer has no control over the price in the market. For the purposes of this discussion this simpler explanation of cost relationships will be sufficient to permit the presentation of the relation of unit cost to the various systems of costing which have been developed to assist management in arriving at decisions to expand, to contract or to remain at the same level of output.

COST RELATIONSHIPS

In order to understand the usefulness of the concepts shown in Fig. 5-1 a few relationships will be discussed. The term full cost is used to denote the sum of variable and fixed costs, whether expressed as a total as in Fig. 5-1 or as average and marginal as in Fig. 5-2. The charts reveal these

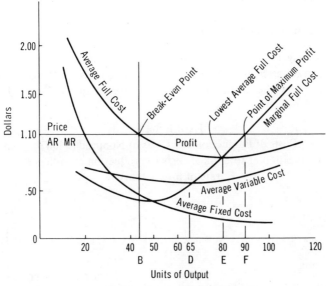

(Based on Data in Appendix Table A-1)

FIG. 5-2. Cost curves—averages.

levels of production, as measured by units of output: (B) at 43 units, shows the break-even point (where average full unit cost is just equal to price), (E) at 80 units, lowest average full cost, and (F) at 90 units, the point of maximum profit where the price determined in the market equals marginal cost. This latter point represents the most profitable situation for the firm. If the 91st item were produced the unit cost would be greater than the unit revenue or price of $1.10. (a competitive firm will not produce an output smaller than D; why not?)

These unit-cost considerations will apply equally well to other portions of the private segment, besides manufacturing. However, the cost of operating a brokerage house or the cost of a salesman for a wholesale drug firm, is more complicated than computing of cost of production of physical goods in a factory. The brokerage house has busy days and dull days; some salesmen will not sell any stock on certain days; the relation between production and cost is not direct as in the case of manufacturing. Salesmen may spend one day or several days in attempting to achieve sales which are consummated days later. In quantitative terms, they seem to have produced nothing, but their efforts may have been effective for future sales, and are thus an investment.

Budgeting and Productive Capacity

Planning future operations of industries, businesses, and individuals in the private segment entails the use of budgets. Most budgets are arranged to show the detail and the total of the prospective receipts, pro-

TABLE 5-1A
Costs of Production and Costs of Nonproduction
(Allocation of total fixed costs to production regardless of rate of production)

	I	II	III
Sales price per unit	$ 1.10	$ 1.10	$ 1.10
Units produced	65	80	90
Sales revenue	$71.50	$88.00	$99.00
Variable costs			
Total	$36.00	$46.00	$56.00
Per unit	.56	.58	.62
Fixed costs			
Total	$20.00	$20.00	$20.00
Per unit	.30	.25	.22
Full costs			
Total	$56.00	$66.00	$76.00
Per unit	.86	.83	.84
Profit per unit	$ .24	$ .27	$ .26
Total profit	15.50	22.00	23.00

spective expenses, and the prospective difference, which if "positive," would be a profit in the case of business or an excess above expenses for an individual.

The business budget should be so designed that a production capacity is predetermined, in order to be able to analyze effectiveness of the use of the long-life assets. The previous example shown in Figs. 5-1 and 5-2 assumed that the total fixed cost of $20 was to be charged to production regardless of output. Also it was shown that the average fixed cost charged to production dropped from 50 cents to 20 cents per unit of output as production increased from 40 units to 100.

If it is desired to isolate and report to management the cost of *not* producing, then a predetermined or standard unit cost for fixed cost should be charged to each unit produced, regardless of the output. The examples in Tables 5-1A and 5-1B illustrate two alternative cost situations.

TABLE 5-1B

Costs of Production and Costs of Nonproduction
(Allocation of fixed costs to production at a fixed rate per unit.)

	IV	V	VI
Sales price per unit	$ 1.10	$ 1.10	$ 1.10
Units produced	65	80	90
Sales revenue	$71.50	$88.00	$99.00
Variable costs			
Total	$36.00	$46.00	$56.00
Per unit	.56	.58	.62
Fixed costs			
(Assume capacity of 80 units therefore $\frac{\$20.}{80}$ − .25 cost per unit)			
Total	$16.25	$20.00	$22.50
Per unit	.25	.25	.25
Full costs			
Total	52.25	66.00	78.50
Per unit	.81	.83	.87
Profit per unit	.29	.27	.23
Total profit before absorption of fixed costs	19.25	22.00	20.50
Under or (over) absorbed fixed costs			
15 units at 25¢	3.75		
None at 25¢		none	
10 units at 25¢			(2.50)
Final profit (same as in case A of total absorption of fixed costs but the detail of cost shown to management)	$15.50	$22.00	$23.00

Allocation of Total Fixed Costs to Production (Regardless of
   Rate of Production)

This is shown in Table 5-1A with total fixed cost of $20 charged to production regardless of whether 65, 80, or 90 units were produced. The unit full cost, shown in Case II, when 80 units were produced, was 83 cents, which was the lowest average full cost of the three cases.

Allocation of Fixed Costs to Production at a Fixed
   Rate Per Unit

In this case, shown in Table 5-1B, the "capacity" has been determined to be 80 units of production because the plant was designed to operate normally at that rate. Since total fixed cost was stated to be $20, the unit fixed cost is 25 cents. This amount is to be charged to production for each unit produced.

In Case IV, when 65 units were produced at 25 cents unit fixed cost, then only $16.25 of the $20 was allocated or "absorbed" and $3.75 was the cost of *not* producing. In contrast to Case IV is Case I, discussed above, with the entire $20 being allocated at 30 cents per unit. Advising management of the cost of *not producing* shows additional information for making intelligent decisions. Case V, with production equal to capacity, has the entire fixed cost allocated to production. Case VI is an example of operation beyond normal capacity with a gain of $2.50 or 10 units above capacity at 25 cents per unit.

Standard Cost Systems

Table 5-1B discussed above, shows a standard rate of fixed costs which permit management to review the results of the extra cost of *not* using fixed assets at their normal capacity. This could result from lack of sales volume or from poor internal management. The next step is to develop standards for all types of cost, including each of the variable costs, permitting management to compare the results to the goal or standard set in advance. These goals may be set in dollars or in quantities of goods. In the private segment the profit incentive encourages this degree of accuracy in the reporting to management. The differences between standard and actual are called "variances," and it is the amount and percentage of variance above and below standard that interests management. This permits decisions about change to be made more intelligently.

Direct-Costing Systems

A departure from the full cost, which included the write-off to production cost of fixed (sometimes called "period" costs), is known as *direct costing.* Only the variable costs are charged to cost of sales or included in inventory at the end of the period. True, in the short run only the direct or variable costs need be covered, but in the long run both variable and fixed must be covered. Also in the long run both types become variable when buildings become obsolete. In the direct-costing system, all fixed costs are written off against income each time period.

GOVERNMENT AND TAX-EXEMPT SEGMENTS

In so far as these segments produce commodities, the analysis discussed above for the private segment is comparable. However, most of the output of government consists of services, which are not easily measurable quantitatively. For example, in local government the efficiency of the fire department is not measured by the number of fires it fights nor the number of calls that it answers. In fact it is the converse—no fires at all would probably be a perfect work record. The firemen might spend time in preventive work, which could result in lower cost of insurance to the citizens. At the state level one could use standard-cost systems for determining net cost of maintaining each prisoner in the penitentiary, but the significant result of money spent for police, attorneys general, and prisons is the reduction of crime, not the unit cost of punishment. Even though unit costs may not be as important in government, the development and use of the budget is very important. Budgets are very useful in government as a guide in planning what to spend in future periods and also as a check on current expenditures, but the real question is what should the budgeted amount be? In other words, what amounts of money will accomplish a certain goal?

PART III

ACCOUNTING
TECHNIQUES
AND TACTICS

Chapter **6**

How To Choose Appropriate Accounting Procedures

The gathering of data to produce the reports needed involves many systems. These range from the traditional cigar box for cash and desk-top skewer file to the latest electronic data-processing machines that operate at unbelievably high speeds (and may make mistakes at equally high speeds).

SINGLE-ENTRY SYSTEM

If the amounts put into the cash box were recorded when received and the amounts taken out and spent were recorded, one would have the beginning of a "single-entry" bookkeeping system and it would be known as a "cash basis."

If some of the cash were spent for a cash register, to eliminate the cigar box, the system becomes a "modified cash basis," as the cash register cannot be written off to expense in one year when it will last several years.

DOUBLE-ENTRY SYSTEM

Development

Like many other artifacts, records of commercial contracts have been found in the ruins of Babylon. These may have been entered into as long ago as 3000 B.C. Quite extensive accounts were kept of farms and estates in Greece and Rome. Joseph and Mary were returning to Bethlehem to be counted for tax purposes when Christ was born. The first record of "double-entry" accounting was around A.D. 1340 in Genoa, Italy, and the first manual on the subject was written in 1458, by the Italian Cortrugli, followed by a more complete volume, including a detailed discussion of debits and credits, by another Italian, Luca Pacioli.

The first text to be written in the United States appeared in 1796 and hundreds have been published since. The history of accounting reflects the changes in business, industry, and government in the intervening years.

Procedure

If one takes into account the amounts "owed to us" and the "amounts we owe" and calls the increase in "accounts receivable" *income* and the increase in "accounts payable" *expense,* then one has developed an "accrual system." If at the same time one wishes to record changes in ownership, one adds the "ownership accounts" and one has a "double-entry" system. This means that when he invests a dollar, he records the dollar as cash, which is an *asset,* and also records that dollar as *capital,* which is ownership. When goods are purchased on "credit," the goods become an *"asset"* and the obligation becomes a "liability." These are the three parts of the first *accounting equation,*

$$\text{Assets} - \text{Liabilities} = \text{Net Worth}$$

This is why the Position Statement is often called a "Balance Sheet," because in a double-entry system the two sides of the equation are in balance, but since this is so by definition it is nonsignificant. If, for example, an item is sold for cash at a gross profit (more than cost) then cash is increased, inventory is decreased, and ownership or net worth is increased, but the balance is maintained as the changes in the accounts were equal in amount on both sides of the equation.

In order to sort the parts of the transaction, a shorthand language has been developed wherein such a sale as that above would be analyzed as a *debit* to cash and a *credit* to inventory and also a *credit* to ownership. Thus a second accounting equation has been developed: *debits* equal *credits.*

Chart of Accounts

In order to reflect all of the various aspects of financial activity, the person designing the system uses a Chart of Accounts, which also makes possible simplified record-keeping in that each part of the transaction is numbered. The groups used are often as follows:

100   Assets
200   Liabilities
300   Net worth, ownership or "capital"
400   Income
500   Expenses

Journals and Ledgers

To record the financial activities, when they first occur, the *journal* (from Latin, *diurnalis,* French *journal,* an account of daily transactions) is used in chronological order. The first step in summarizing takes place when totals by account numbers are posted to the *ledger,* which contains each of the *accounts.* At the end of an accounting period—that is, a month, a quarter, or a year—the financial statements are prepared from the accounts in the ledger, after adjustments, if any are necessary.

Retention of Records

As activities become more complex it seems that the volume of records increases in more than a proportional amount, necessitating a system of *retention* or the concomitant *destruction* of records. To determine the length of time of retention, the statute of limitations under the various laws must be considered. For example, certain items are no longer valid after seven years. The Internal Revenue Service can audit the past three years (except under special circumstances, as explained in Chapter 11). Hence the retention of records depends on the use of records for legal liability, and also whether the same information is duplicated in other records.

Chapter 7

How To Use Accounting as a Tool for Decision Making

The effectiveness of a decision may be measured by investigating whether or not the desired end was accomplished. This may be difficult because of other factors interfering between the time of the decision and the time its effectiveness is to be measured. For example, in the private segment it may be considered advisable to expand a plant to manufacture a given quantity of consumer goods. Based on the facts presented and the estimates about the future, the decision to invest is made and carried out. If a competitor later improves his product which cut in on sales, a lower volume results. Thus despite careful forecasting and a competent decision, results may be nonetheless disappointing.

HOW TO COLLECT AND STORE RELEVANT DATA

The first step in collecting data is compiling a set of adequate definitions of the categories concerned so that there can be no confusion on the part of the reporters. In the private segment there is some confusion in revenue between taxable and nontaxable sales, and there is always the possibility of confusion in classification of expenses unless they are carefully designated. In the commercial world there are various manuals of accounts published by trade associations, each adapted to specific needs.

In the semipublic field of the public utilities, the regulatory bodies publish recommended accounts and procedures. For local governments the National Municipal Finance Officers Association and the state associations publish recommended systems of accounts.

The collection of data usually begins with manual recording. The data may be transposed to punch cards or put on tapes or disks for tabulation by electronic machine accounting—assuming there is a sufficient volume of transactions to warrant the use of high-speed machines.

The intermediate step .in mechanization, if the volume is not high, is manually operated accounting machines. These have a disadvantage in that they cannot automatically store data to be retrieved by the machine itself.

If electronic machines are used and the program is properly designed, the machine can store and tabulate the details of the transactions, prepare reports, and print them out as a final product. The rapidity of the operation is important to all segments of the economy, but the interpretation of the results is still a human function and management still has to make the decisions based on the reports rendered by the machine.

HOW ACCOUNTING "PRINCIPLES" RELATE TO ECONOMIC "THEORIES"

A definition of accounting and economics will be reviewed before the relation between the two disciplines is considered:

> Accounting is a broad term that denotes certain theories, behavioral assumptions, measurement rules and procedures for collecting and reporting useful information concerning the activities and objectives of an organization . . . Accounting consists of procedures for recording, classifying and interpreting selected experiences of an enterprise to promote effective administration[1]

And again,

> Economics is the study of how men and society choose, with or without the use of money, to employ *scarce* productive resources to produce various commodities over time and distribute them for consumption, now and in the future, among various people and groups in society[2]

According to the above definition, accounting involves the study of useful information concerning the activities and objectives of an organization. This includes—and justifiably so—a value judgment as to usefulness. Why would anyone gather useless information? Yet what is meant by usefulness—usefulness to *whom*? In some cases information concerning a particular organization, in the private segment of the economy, could be useless to the owners or managers of the concern, but would be useful to

[1]Carl Thomas Devine, *Encyclopedia Britannica*, Vol. 1, 1965, p. 78.
[2]Paul A. Samuelson, *Economics, An Introductory Analysis,* 6th ed., McGraw-Hill, New York, 1964, p. 5.

an economist studying the society as a whole. The definition of economics implies that the data necessary to study the allocation of scarce factors is available, but this is not always so.

The term *theories* in relation to *principles* is of interest, as the independent accountant's letter reporting on his verification includes the words "in accordance with generally accepted accounting principles." For accounting purposes the words *theory* and *principle* can be used synonymously. Each of the principles, therefore, serves as a guide in handling the data which are gathered and reported on for the individual organization. This applies to analysis of past data as well as to data used for planning the future.

In economics, data can be applied, to some extent, to test the validity of the theories. There are two major areas in economic theory—macroeconomics and microeconomics. In macroeconomics an attempt is made to develop theories which are of some usefulness in the administration of the economy as a whole. Such theories should be subject, in part, to verification by the use of statistical data. Microeconomics is the study of households, business firms, and industries which constitute the constituent parts of the economic whole.

Verification of economic theories is difficult because so many variables are involved. The theories are constructed by assuming other things being equal, or by assuming that certain items are constant. When data is related to the theories, items cannot always be held constant in the real world.

A principle has been defined as "a crystallization of ideas into a clear verbal statement of a significant relationship."[3] A major accounting principle, expressed in 1938, was stated as follows:

> The distinction between capital and income, which everyone recognizes and the economist attempts to state with refined accuracy, is fundamental in accounting.[4]

This first principle is equally significant in all three segments—private, government, and nonprofit. It may appear more important in the private segment, especially when taxes are based on income. In government it is even more important to know which items are capital and which are income to be expended in the year concerned. Another form of the

---

[3] A. C. Littleton, *Structure of Accounting Theory*, American Accounting Association, 1953, p. 23.
[4] Sanders, Hatfield and Moore, *Statement of Accounting Principles*, American Institute of Accountants, 1938, p. 1.

same principle states that there should be a *matching of current expenses with current revenue,* in order that capital not be depleted.

Other principles, derived from the major principle above, are, second the *going-concern* principle. This assumes that the organization under discussion will continue and is not in the process of liquidation. In the private segment this is important because the value of assets (machinery and buildings, for example) would be quite different if a liquidation, piece by piece, were contemplated, rather than a continuation of the firm as a going concern. Governments are always assumed to be "going concerns."

The fact that accounting involves the recording of quantitative and qualitative data has led to the development of the third principle of *disclosure.* This involves a value judgment on the part of the accountant that nothing of significance to any report has been omitted. In the case of an annual report of a business or agency of government or a tax-exempt organization, this means that all significant facts were either reduced to numerical data or they have been discussed in the written report. Related to this principle of disclosure is the fourth, that of *materiality.* Certain items are so small, relative to the total, that either they are combined with others or omitted. However, certain items, though small in numerical size, are important to the report so that they will be disclosed as a note, or reported in the covering opinion letter. Here the size is not the determinant of importance.

A fifth principle of accounting is that of *consistency* from period to period. The period is usually a year or fraction of a year. As most accounting data is on an historical cost basis, the sixth and final principle of *conservatism* holds. Since the value of the dollar fluctuates, historical costs can be misleading as to market value.

The significance of the "principles" is shown in the examples of accountants' report letters, in Chapter 10, as each includes the term "generally accepted accounting principles." As yet the profession is not agreed on a specific list of principles, nor the precise meaning of "generally accepted."

A recent writer has summarized the application of several of the principles as follows:

> In a given economic situation, accountants wish to account conservatively, objectively, and with full disclosure, for an accounting entity which is a going concern, for a uniform period of time, all the material financial facts on a basis which is consistent from period to period.[5]

[5] Donald A. Corbin, *Accounting and Economic Decisions,* Dodd, Mead, 1964, p. 234.

Chapter 8

How To Interpret Financial Reports

Financial reports are required in order to manage the business properly. Many personable entrepreneurs come to grief because they fail to make proper use of data available to them. The concern may also come to grief when the accountants do not provide data in the right form. Accounting is a means rather than an end. Management must instruct accountants to be creative in presenting material. However, if management is disposed to examine records available and the accountants keep them properly, then the firm has the material for the next step so as to illuminate and guide its policies.

LIMITATIONS

Financial reports for one year only, even if shown in great detail, are of limited value because no clue is given as to changes. If several years are shown, a trend may be discerned that is useful in estimating the future. Likewise reports of only one organization offer no basis for the study of comparative efficiency. If reports of several similar organizations are available, comparisons are possible. Such comparisons are essential in a competitive economy and desireable in measuring governmental efficiency.

STATISTICAL TOOLS THAT HELP IN ANALYSIS

For either Position Statement data or Income Statement data, two main types of comparisons are possible: vertical or horizontal. In the case of the horizontal, it is customary to prepare a series of data and convert them to percentages using one year as the base of 100 percent. Then it can be stated that, two years later, sales were 14 percent of the base year.

Similar comparisons can be made for each of the items in the statements. Also comparisons between organizations can be of some significance. For example, a decision might be based on the fact that the sales of Company A were 142 percent of the base year and those of Company B were 165 percent. If data for several companies were available a secondary calculation could oe made and an average computed to show the typical increase or decrease over the base year.

Vertical analysis for the Position Statement involves the assumption that the total assets or liabilities equal 100 percent and then the component parts are expressed as percentages of the total. In the case of the Income Statement it is usual to let net sales equal 100 percent and then express the cost of sales, gross income, expenses, and net income as percentages of net sales. In a certain industry, for example, the rent expense as a percent of sales could be computed for each firm and averages calculated.

In the private segment an additional procedure is to compute certain ratios in order to compare results of different organizations. The ratio of current assets to current debts and the ratio of net profits to sales, are two of the many used to make decisions. Some ratios are useful in analyzing the static position and some for the changes in income. A national credit-rating firm publishes annually 14 ratios for each of 125 lines of business, including retailing, wholesaling, manufacturing, and construction.[1] A caution is in order about the inherent danger in the use of ratios. Sometimes a large percentage change in an item, relatively small in amount of dollars, may be misleading. For example, in an Income Statement a 10 percent increase in an item of $100,000 is significant while a 100 percent increase in an item of $100 *may* have no real significance in the operation of the enterprise.

In the business segment the study of the changes in ratios from year to year or month to month gives management guides for decisions.

In the local government field analogous measures are available, such as the cost per mile to sweep streets, the cost of police protection per thousand persons, or the rate of tax delinquency.

In the tax-exempt segment there are published averages of many costs, such as the cost per day of hospital care, daily cost per child in an institution, cost of feeding the destitute in underdeveloped countries, or the cost of overhead related to the collection of donations in a charitable organization—sometimes so great as to discourage donors!

[1] Dun and Bradstreet, Inc., *Key Business Ratios in 125 Lines,* New York. Annually.

Chapter 9

Source and Application of Funds; Special Reports

The Source and Application of Funds report combines the data shown on the Income Statement with the data on two Position Statements, one for the beginning of the income period and one for the end of the period. This report is often known colloquially as the "where got" and "where gone" statement.

The Source and Application of Funds could be equally useful to management or to the owners of business or to the electorate. The word "funds," as used in this section, means *working capital,* which is current assets less current liabilities. An alternate method is sometimes employed and a report prepared showing the Source and Application of Cash. In the latter case the detailed changes in each of the current assets and current liabilities are shown. Usually the funds statement is sufficient, without showing all of the detail involved in the cash statement. Table 9-1 shows an example of Source and Application of Funds in the private segment, for a period of one year, for a corporation.

The two sources of funds were income of $8,275, before depreciation and amortization, and $45,000 raised by increasing bonded debt. (The expenses of depreciation, depletion, or amortization are always added back to net income after taxes, because these amounts were not paid out in cash. Depreciation, at the end of any period reflects an increase in both the depreciation expense and depreciation allowance.)

The application of the funds is mainly payments to shareholders, purchase of new machinery, investment in a subsidiary (a corporation owned by the parent corporation) and a net increase in working capital of $10,000. This latter change could be either an increase in current assets or a decrease in current liabilities, or both. In this example the change is all in the increase in current assets, as it is assumed that current liabilities did not change.

TABLE 9-1
Source and Application of Funds—196X
Private Segment—Corporation Example
(Based on data in Appendix Table A-4)

Source
Net income after taxes (Table 3-1) . . . . $ 4,000
Add back—depreciation . . . . $ 3,975
      —amortization   300   4,275

Adjusted net income   8,275
Increase in bonds payable—new debt   45,000

Total source $53,275

Application (or uses)
Dividends paid to stockholders $ 3,100
New machinery . . . . $ 2,000
New buildings   20,000
New land   8,000   30,000

Investment in subsidiary   10,000
Payment of "other liabilities" 175 $43,275

Increase in working capital   10,000

Total application $53,275

SOURCE AND APPLICATION OF FUNDS—GOVERNMENT

As most government agencies do not prepare adequate Position Statements they are unable to prepare Statements of the Source and Application of Funds, similar to those now widely used in the private segment. In the municipal examples of Position Statements included in this book, Tables 2-4 and A-5; certain modifications from usual practice have been made. The long-life assets and inventory of materials and supplies have been included and the statements are on an accrual basis, except that no depreciation of long-life assets is shown.

An examination of Table 9-2, the statement for Cityville, U.S.A., shows that the source of funds includes an increase in bonded debt of $100,000 in order to erect a building, an increase in special assessments of $91,000 for a new project not yet completed, increases in reserves, increase of $15,100 in the unappropriated surplus (from the Revenue and

TABLE 9-2
Source and Application of Funds
Cityville, U.S.A.
(For Year Ended June 30,196X)
(Based on data in Appendix Tables A-5 and A-6)

Source ("Where got")
Liabilities
  Bonds payable
    General bonded debt* $100,000
    Special Assessment bonds   91,000
                                                                              ─────────
                                                                               191,000
  Interest payable future years*   38,000

Reserves
  Encumbrances   17,450
  Retirement sinking-fund bonds   10,400
  Appropriations—unencumbered balance   5,000

Net Worth
  Unappropriated surplus (see Revenue
    and Expenditure Statement).   15,100
  Property Fund—net worth   100,000
                                                                              ─────────
                                                                              $376,950
                                                                              ═════════

Application ("Where gone")

Working capital† . . . . $ 39,150
Investments   9,800
Special assessments receivable   90,000
Buildings constructed   100,000
"Amount available and to be provided
  for interest and retirement of bonds"*   138,000
                                                                              ─────────
                                                                              $376,950
                                                                              ═════════

*In municipal accounting the future interest payable on bonds ($38,000) is
shown as well as the principal of the bonds ($100,000), and these two items are
offset by an equal amount shown here as an Application of Funds ($138,000).

  †Working Capital

	6/30/6X⁻¹	6/30/6X	Increase (decrease)
Current assets	$156,000	$224,050	$68,050
Current liabilities	80,000	108,900	28,900
	$ 76,000	$115,150	$39,150

Expenditures Statement), and an increase in the Property Fund net worth of $100,000.

The application or use of the funds shows an increase in working capital of $39,150, an increase in investments of $9,800, special assessment receivable increase of $90,000, and buildings for $100,000. Thus the changes in the financial position of a government agency, such as a city, can be readily seen when this statement is prepared.

CASH-FLOW ANALYSIS

In order to plan in advance for short-term bank loans for commercial concerns, an analysis is prepared of expected cash receipts and disbursements, based on past experience but tempered with an estimate of the future. This report is usually prepared by months or quarters. First the various receipts, cash and sales collections on accounts receivable, or (in the case of government) collections on taxes receivable are tabulated, and then the cash disbursements (including payments on accounts payable, cash purchases, and wages payable) are estimated. Thus management can determine whether or not it faces a shortage of cash in a certain month or quarter. If a shortage is estimated, the firm or agency can plan its short-term loans in advance rather than wait until the need is urgent. Before a loan is obtained, the banker often wishes to see a cash-flow analysis. This helps him to forecast when there will be an excess of cash available to repay part or all of the loan.

TIME-SERIES ANALYSIS

One Position Statement or one Income Statement is not of much value in long-range planning for the future as trends are not discernible. However, a series of records even for five years allows certain key figures such as the amount of working capital or the ratio of current assets to current liabilities to be plotted, and may reveal general tendencies. The relationship can be in direct proportions, represented by a straight line—or it may be a curvilinear relationship.

Figure 9-1 shows an example of business conditions together with an extrapolation of both a straight line and a curve. The period chosen for the data as well as the method to be used can affect the results. Once the period is chosen and the type of relationship determined, the curve or straight line can be fitted mathematically. Most economic data is not

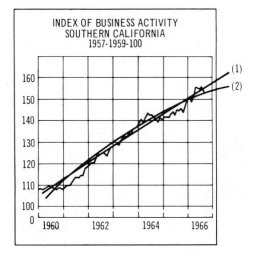

INDEX OF BUSINESS ACTIVITY
SOUTHERN CALIFORNIA
1957-1959-100

FIG. 9-1. Time-series analysis. (1) Straight-line projection into the future, which shows an equal amount of change each year indefinitely. (2) Curved-line projection into the future which, in this case assumes more than an equal amount of change per year during the early years and less than an equal amount of change during the later years when the curve flattens. (Source: *Monthly Summary of Business Conditions in Southern California*, Security First National Bank, Economic Research Division, October 1, 1966.)

reducible to such a high degree of precision, especially since arbitrary decisions have to be made about the period to be studied and the type of relationship to be assumed.

WHEN CAN SPECIAL REPORTS HELP

After the data has been gathered by the accounting process it can be rearranged and sorted in ways to be of special assistance to management.

The basic reports show "stock" and "flow" in the Position Statement and the Income Statement. Certain other reports can be prepared from data already gathered such as the Source and Application of Funds and a Time-Series Analysis.

Information, in addition to the data gathered for the basic reports, is often needed in order to complete the analysis to make adequate decisions. In addition to "quantitative" data usually gathered, it is often necessary to obtain "qualitative" data in order to control the quality of the output.

Quality-Control Report

In most of this book the values discussed have been quantitative in nature. However, the *quality* of the product or service is vital in all three segments of the economy. In the private sector the goods sold are not paid for unless they pass inspection. This inspection may mean adherence to very rigid standards where a manufacturer is working to producer specifications but somewhat looser standards for retail goods. Testing the product to see if it meets the specification is sometimes difficult; the tensile strength of steel is a good example since the ultimate test is to strain a piece until it breaks after which it is not salable. Sampling techniques have to be developed where a few items of each batch, of presumably homogenous items, are destroyed by testing. If they pass satisfactorily, the manufacturer concludes that the rest of the items in the batch are satisfactory for sale.

As the government and tax-exempt segment of the economy provide services rather than physical products, the application of quality control is not as simple. Measures have been developed to judge the services performed quantitatively, but the judgment as to the quality of services performed by government employees will probably remain an intangible. However, when the quality is bad the supervisors usually hear about it, even though it is not statistically measurable—except perhaps in number of complaints. If these supervisors are responsible to the elected officials, the problems are usually remedied sooner or later.

Time and Motion Studies

In applying the factors of production in the most efficient and economical manner, it is often advisable to make a time and motion study of the particular activity. By means of breaking down an activity into its component parts it is possible to devise more efficient means of achieving the stated goal. The application is easiest in the private segment, especially in the manufacturing of relatively standard items. In this case the operator of a machine is timed as to each part of his activity and goals are set which make possible quantitative measures above or below the goal. Many times the procedures are changed after the study because of exposure of inefficient procedures.

The same type of study, resulting in time schedules for each part of an activity, has been done in office procedures. This also may result in greater efficiency. Obviously the output must pass inspection or the process would only encourage a larger volume of unsatisfactory work, which is no gain to the business. Similar procedures have been applied to the government segment and to the tax-exempt segment of the economy, but difficulties arise when the measurement techniques are applied to personnel problems, such as an interview by a social worker in an agency, or a visit by a nurse of a tax-exempt community organization. These activities are not often reducible to measurable quantities when the person involved may justifiably need to spend more time on one case than another.

Chapter 10

When Professional Judgment Is Required

The accountant can make several contributions to management to assist in the decision-making process. The framework of record-keeping must be devised so that the reports produced will be meaningful, and up-to-date. The accountant also makes a contribution by rearranging and summarizing data. He interprets this information for management and renders advice to assist in choosing between alternative paths of action. If he is in an independent position (not an officer, owner, or employee) he may be engaged to perform the functions of authentication and verification.

These professional attributes are useful in all three segments of the economy.

AUDITING—INDEPENDENT VERIFICATION

Many men and women in the accounting profession are employed by organizations as treasurers, controllers, directors of finance (municipalities), administrators, or other titles signifying responsibility for financial matters *within* the organization. Others are independent consultants who work *outside* of the organization for several clients, and who because of their independence can render an opinion on the status of the financial affairs expressed in reports prepared by the first group. This is called the *audit* function. Perhaps it should be called Independent Verification. These consultants also advise on government matters and represent their clients before the agencies concerned. These may include the Internal Revenue Service (income and other taxes), Securities and Exchange Commission (issuance of stocks and bonds), Federal Power Commission (setting rates for utilities), and state agencies of many types. These consultants also assist with internal matters including operations research, installation of cost systems, data processing, decisions as to expansion, reorganization and insurance.

Many of the above services are useful to all the segments of the economy, government and tax-exempt organizations, as well as firms in the private segment. All segments need the advice of consultants in many fields.

and Company

Certified Public Accountants
Cityville, USA

Board of Directors,
XYZ Corporation
Cityville, U.S.A.

We have examined the consolidated financial statements of
the XYZ Corporation and subsidiaries for the year ended
December 31, 196X. Our examination was made in accordance
with generally accepted auditing standards, and, accordingly,
included such tests of the accounting records and such
other auditing procedures as we considered necessary in
the circumstances. We also made a similar examination of
the financial statements for the year ended December 31,
196X-1.

In our opinion, the accompanying consolidated statements
of financial position, income and stockholders' equity, and
source and application of funds present fairly the financial
position of XYZ Corporation and subsidiaries at December
31, 196x and 196X, and the results of their operations and
the source and application of funds for the years then ended,
in conformity with generally accepted accounting principles
applied on a consistent basis.

                    ABC AND COMPANY
                    Certified Public Accountants

Cityville, U.S.A.
February 15, 196X+1

FIG. 10-1. Auditor's report—private segment (corporation which
owns subsidiary corporations).

The types of opinions given by the auditor after he has completed his verifications are:

1. No-exception report letter (unqualified)
2. Exception report letter (qualified)
3. Disclaimer of an opinion
4. Adverse opinion

(These four different possible results of an audit are delineated by the individual state boards of accountancy, the state professional societies, and the American Institute of Certified Public Accountants.)

D E F **and Company**   Certified Public Accountants
Cityville, USA

The Honorable City Council
Cityville, U.S.A.

We have examined the balance sheets of the various
funds of the City of Cityville as of December 31,
196X and the statements of revenues and expenses and
fund equities for the year then ended. Our examination was made in accordance with generally accepted
auditing standards, and accordingly included such
tests of the accounting records and such other auditing procedures as we considered necessary in the circumstances.

In accordance with established accounting practices
for municipalities no provision has been made for
depreciation of physical properties other than properties of the water fund, which is a self-supporting
unit, nor is accrued interest on bonds payable taken
into account.

In our opinion, the accompanying balance sheets and
statements of revenues and expenses and fund equities
present fairly the financial position of the various
funds of the City of Cityville at December 31, 196X,
and the results of operations for the year then ended,
in conformity with accounting practices used by municipalities, applied on a basis consistent with that
of the preceding year.

DEF and Company
Certified Public Accountants

Cityville, U.S.A.
February 15, 196X+1

FIG. 10-2. Auditor's report—government segment (municipal example).

The completion of the year-end audit by the independent accountant and the rendering of an opinion, *with no exceptions* (or "unqualified opinion" in technical terms), assures the owners, whether they are stockholders, in the case of a commercial corporation, the taxpayers in the case

GHI **and Company**

Certified Public Accountants
Cityville, USA

To the Board of Directors of
St. Swithin's-in-the-Field
Cityville, U.S.A.

We have examined the statement of financial position of
St. Swithin's-in-the-Field (a Pennsylvania nonprofit
corporation) as of December 31, 196X, and the related
statements of income, expenditures and changes in fund
balances for the year then ended. Our examination was
made in accordance with generally accepted auditing
standards, and accordingly included such tests of the
accounting records and such other auditing procedures as
we considered necessary in the circumstances.

Accurals of income and expenses as of December 31, 196X,
have not been included in the statement of financial position
since the church maintains its books on a cash basis. Income
due but not received at the beginning and end of the year do
not differ materially in amount. There were no material
expenditures budgeted, but unpaid, at the beginning or end
of the year, which have not been provided for in the statements.

In our opinion the accompanying financial statements present
fairly the financial position of St. Swithin's-in-the-Field
at December 31, 196X, and the income, expenditures and
changes in fund balances for the year then ended in conformity with accounting principles followed generally by similar
institutions, which were applied on a basis consistent with
that of the preceding year.

                         GHI AND COMPANY
                         Certified Public Accountants

February 15, 196X+1

FIG. 10-3. Auditor's report—tax-exempt segment.

of government agencies, or donors in the case of tax-exempt corporations, that the report "fairly presents" the financial activities of the year concerned. The opinion does not state that the management was efficient or wise, but that the report fairly portrays what happened. It does not state that the decisions made were necessarily the "right" ones for the organization. Examples of audit report letters for three different types of organizations are illustrated in Figs. 10-1, 10-2, and 10-3.

The exception report letter is written when *there are exceptions* taken to the quality of the entire report on financial position. Such an exception might arise because the client would not permit inventory to be counted, but since the value of the inventory was not a significant amount relative to total assets, a *qualified* opinion could be rendered. However, if significant items could not be verified, or other audit procedures not carried out, then the independent auditor must *disclaim* an opinion and state his reasons.

When the auditor finds something wrong, he must disclose what he finds, even if it is detrimental to the organization being audited. This is called an *adverse opinion.* The author has found only one example of an adverse opinion rendered by an independent auditor. In practice the auditor often uses the threat of an adverse opinion to persuade the client to make certain changes. If the disputed matter is one of classification or computation, then the threat of an adverse opinion may be dropped when appropriate changes are made, but if it is a "fact" which, of course, cannot be changed, then an adverse opinion would have to be rendered.

TAX ADVICE: AVOID, NOT EVADE

Avoidance of taxes by planning transactions to minimize taxes is ethical and legal. Evasion of taxes by any means is illegal. As there are many disputed points in the field of taxation, some finally settled by the Supreme Court of the United States, there are always items which are successfully challenged by the taxpayer and by the Internal Revenue Service so that changes are made in the amount of taxes.

The consultant's work in the tax field is not limited to the private segment, as the government agencies are the recipients of the taxes and the tax-exempts are recipients of contributions.

Of the many aspects to the provision of tax advice, the most important is *timing.* In most cases the alternatives exist only before the transaction is consummated. Some of the transactions are of short-term importance, such as selling for cash or on the installment plan, and some are long-term in consequence, such as the choice of type of business organization—partnership or corporation.

The person giving the advice must be well trained. There are more than 8,000 sections in the Internal Revenue Code, besides voluminous regulations, rulings, and court cases. There are state income tax regulations as most of the states and a few cities have an income tax as a source of revenue.

TAX SAVINGS VS. GOOD MANAGEMENT

In planning transactions so that income taxes are minimized, it is possible to develop an unsound situation financially. For example, an installment sale, where the payments are made over a period of several tax years, reduces the total tax and spreads the tax burden over those years by having part of the income in a lower bracket. (This does not take into account the loss of interest on money received at a later date.) This reduction in tax is possible by the seller accepting less than 30 percent down payment. However, it may be imprudent for the seller to accept less than 30 percent because of the risk involved that the buyer may never pay the balance and the property would have to be reclaimed by the seller.

CONDUIT RULE

Related to the choice of type of organization is what might be called the "conduit" rule, as the income may flow through several legal entities before finally being taxed.

The partnership is the first example as there is no income tax, Federal or state, paid with a partnership return, but each partner pays his own tax on income as reported on the return. The beneficiary of a trust is in a similar position, as there may be several types of income flowing through the trust. Expenses may also be reported by the trust that are deductible by the individual beneficiary.

PROFESSIONAL QUALIFICATIONS OF PERSONNEL

Most of the people handling accounting problems today are college graduates and many have advanced degrees, but there is a problem with the name of the activity in common terminology of educational systems. The often dull "bookkeeping" course in high schools is a so-called "terminal" course, and does not count for college credit, nor is it taken by college preparatory students. Very few high schools teach economics. If more did, it might encourage more people to enter the field of accounting, earlier in their college career. College training is valuable for accountants, especially courses in accounting, economics, law, government statistics and, of course, a general education including history, science, and the humanities. Several states now require a college degree in order to sit for the Certified Public Accountant examination. At present all 50 states use the uniform examination prepared and graded by the American Institute of Certified Public Accountants.

PART IV

TAXES

Chapter 11

What Kinds of Taxes Are Paid?

Taxes will be briefly examined in this chapter, as they are most important in accounting. Other types of governmental revenue arbitrarily are set by law and are not flexible or reduced by computation by accountants in accordance with accounting principles. As a citizen the accountant is interested in public debates as to the efficacy and equity of the three major types of taxes. Decisions of the managers of the private segment to move from one government jurisdiction to another are often said to be based on tax considerations. The pricing of products is affected directly by the imposition of a sales tax and indirectly by other taxes.

TYPES OF TAXES

Basically three types of tax affect the businessman and must be accounted for:

1. Tax on business transactions
2. Tax on income
3. Tax on property

A sales tax, which is a tax on business transactions, may be imposed at several points in the stream, on the consumer, the retailer, the wholesaler, or the manufacturer. If it is assessed on the retailer, it is often said to be passed on to the customer. Here it is usually clearly shown as an addition to the sales price. The amount of a new sales tax absorbed by the seller or borne by the buyer would depend upon the nature of the demand and supply curves of the commodity concerned. If sales decline after the imposition of a tax, the seller is penalized by less sales income.

The usual accounting statement shows the sales tax collected as a payable to the government agency to whom it is due. The other sales taxes, often called *indirect* or *excise* taxes, are assessed on raw materials entering into the manufacture and likewise may be added to the ultimate cost of production. They may serve to reduce the net income of one of the persons in the series of transactions. In any event the sales taxes, other than the last retail tax, are not reflected directly in the seller's financial statement. The theoretical discussion of the burden of the different taxes and the possible shifting of this burden must be explored elsewhere.

The income tax, either personal or corporate, is not a tax on each transaction but one assessed only if income exceeds expenses beyond allowable exemptions. A change in the rates of income tax alters the net income retained by the business organization or by the individual. Under certain circumstances a business can shift part of an increase in income tax to the consumer in the form of higher prices.

From an accounting point of view the effective rate of income taxes, both Federal and state (most states have an income tax), is vital in determining under which form a business should be organized, i.e., proprietorship, partnership, or corporation. Determining the proper form often requires projections of future income, which is difficult to do because of the uncertainties in the business world.

Some cities now have a gross payroll tax, often called an income tax, but it differs from the official income tax in that there are no deductions or exemptions. This tax is similar to a sales tax, if it is assumed that the employees spend *all* of their income, a common problem!

Property taxes constitute a significant cost of doing business. (There are certain property taxes which are not closely related to business, i.e., the gift tax, the estate, or inheritance tax. The Federal and several state governments assess taxes on certain gifts which are transfers of property between living individuals. The estate tax is the Federal tax on the value of property owned by an individual at the time of his death, while the inheritance tax is the name used for a similar tax imposed by the state governments.) Business is assessed property taxes on its real property (land and buildings), personal property (machinery and inventories) and, in some states, on solvent credits or cash in banks and accounts receivable net of accounts payable. The tax on inventories (raw materials and finished goods) assessed on a certain day of the year by several states has disrupted purchasing and shipment procedures and encouraged business to move inventories from one state to another to avoid taxation.

The percentage of gross income devoted to taxes has been increasing and is sufficiently high to make the individual businessman or manager of a corporation vitally interested in the control of government expenditures.

INCOME TAX PROCEDURES

The income tax of the United States and of most of the states is known as a "voluntarily assessed" tax because the individuals or managers of corporations, trusts, or other types of business organizations prepare their own tax returns and calculate the amount of tax due. They often have the assistance of certified public accountants in preparing these returns, but they are considered "voluntary" because the amount of the tax is not computed by a government agency, as is the case in certain other types of taxation.

The Federal income tax is based on the code, as passed by Congress, the regulations of the Commissioner of Internal Revenue, the many administrative rulings of the Internal Revenue Service, and the decisions of the courts. Since it accounts for approximately 40 percent of Federal cash receipts the effect of this tax on the economic system is vital.[1]

Many states have an income tax and some cities have now adopted this method of financing for local government. Much duplication of collection cost and filing cost could be avoided if the state government could employ a fixed percentage of the Federal tax rate.

The amount of income for income tax purposes may be different from that used for financial statement purposes. However, any such difference, for a corporation, is to be explained in a special schedule on the tax return. An example would be the fee paid to obtain financing. If this is a small amount relative to total income, it may be expensed (which means written off) in one year or less; however, if the financing extended over a 20-year period, the fee will have to be prorated on the tax return over the projected life of the loan or 5 percent per year.

There are other situations in which decisions are required in preparing income tax returns and reporting the tax due. In order to be allowed by the government most of these decisions need to be made *before* the transaction takes place, not at the time of reporting the results.

Since 1942 a large portion of the Federal income tax is collected in accordance with a system of withholding by the employer, throughout the year, and forwarded by him to the government. Other persons with income not subject to withholding are required to pay an estimated amount, quarterly, in advance. Even before the withholding system started the employer had reported to the government the amounts of wages paid.

---

[1] Joseph A. Peckman, *Federal Tax Policy*, Brookings Institution, Washington, D. C., 1966.

Several states have adopted a withholding system and others are considering such a method of tax collection.

Social Security Taxes

Social Security Tax is a Federal tax borne equally by the employee and the employer or paid wholly by the self-employed. It is also known as Old Age and Survivors Insurance (OASI), as it is paid back to the individual employee upon retirement and also has benefits for a widow and for minor children. The act which created this system is known as the Federal Insurance Contributions Act, so the tax is usually called FICA.

Unemployment Taxes

Another type of payroll deduction is in connection with the state unemployment insurance (SUI) programs. A deduction from the payroll is made for the disability insurance and the employer pays the state unemployment. Related to this program is the Federal Unemployment Insurance (FUI). In computing the Federal tax, credit is given for the payment of the state tax.

PROPERTY TAXES

Property taxes on real and personal property are not collected on such a voluntary basis as the income taxes, but are based on appraisal, usually made by a representative of local government. The right to appeal, such as to the Board of Tax Appeals in the larger counties in California, is a new and uncertain protection for the taxpayer.

The property tax levied is the result of an appraisal figure and the tax rate in effect. Business inventories, on hand on the lien date, which is the date and time for items to be assessed, are often declared by the owner at a value which is accepted by the assessor. These appraised values are human judgments based on what the property might sell for but which are not fact, only estimates. Because of this situation management has to make decisions to accept or reject these appraised values. As tax rates and appraisals have increased, so has the burden on the business man. Computations need to be more carefully checked before the taxes are paid, since the rate grows larger almost annually.

SALES TAXES

The sales tax is usually assessed on the buyer, but collected by the seller. The tax is a consumer's retail tax which is to be added to the price set by the seller. (Sometimes the tax is said to be absorbed; for example an article sold for $1 including 4 percent tax is in reality the sale of an article priced at approximately 96.15 cents and a 4 percent tax of 3.85 cents. More often it is openly added to the retail price.) In certain states the sales tax reporting involves segregating nontaxable items such as food for home consumption, and services, such as shoe repairing, from the rest of the sales.

As the element of choosing between alternatives is not as involved in computing the sales tax as in the other taxes, the need for decisions is not present. However, decisions must be made in interpreting the codes and regulations governing the collecting agency.

AUDITING OF REPORTS BY GOVERNMENT

All reports rendered to governmental agencies are subject to audit or scrutiny by these agencies. The Internal Revenue Service administers two major types of audits, called *office audit* and *field audit.* In the first case the taxpayer is asked to come to the office with records to verify the income and expense items on his tax return and in the second case the auditor visits the taxpayer's office. In either case the burden of proof, for deductions from income, is on the taxpayer; therefore he must maintain and retain adequate records. In the case of the Federal income tax the statute of limitations is three years from the due date for the returns, April 15, in recent years. (Exceptions in the statute of limitations occur in the cases of fraud, which is "wilful intent to decieve", or when errors are more than 25 percent of the income or expenses).

Other Federal government agencies can audit payroll taxes, state agencies can audit records on sales tax, workmen's compensation, and state unemployment payments.

BIBLIOGRAPHY

Annotated Bibliography

REFERENCES BY PARTS

Part I   Accounting, Wealth, and Income

New York Stock Exchange, *Understanding Financial Statements,* New York, 1965. An explanation in straightforward language of each of the items on corporate financial statements. No charge.

Prudential Insurance Company of America, *Economic Forecast,* 17th Annual edition, 1968. Contains the outlook for the year and charts for 10 years of Gross National Product, government expenditures, family income, and other economic data. No charge.

Simons, Henry C., *Personal Income Taxation,* University of Chicago Press, Chicago, 1937.

Part II   Values and Efficiency

Bursk, Edward C., *New Decision-Making Tools for Managers,* New American Library, Inc., New York, 1963. An inexpensive paperback with articles on applications of new techniques by 25 authors.

Carter, Byron L., *Data Processing for the Small Business,* Macfadden-Bartell, New York, 1966. An inexpensive paperback on applications, opportunities of useful analysis, and limitation of electronic data processing.

Dun and Bradstreet, Inc., *Key Business Ratios in 125 Lines.* Published annually. Contains 14 significant financial ratios for sample firms in each group. Available without charge at 99 Church Street, New York, New York 10007.

Gibbs, George, *Manual For Parish Treasurers,* 2d ed. 1967, Episcopal Diocese of Los Angeles. A presentation of detailed accounting and management procedures for an incorporated church. Contains sample monthly and yearly report forms.

Matz, Adolph, et al., *Cost Accounting,* South-Western Publishing Co. Cincinnati, 1967. Useful for further reference on unit-cost analysis, standard cost procedures, direct-cost systems, and cost reporting for management purposes.

Part III   Accounting Techniques and Tactics

American Accounting Association, *A Statement of Basic Accounting Theory,* Evanston, Ill. 1966.

American Institute of Certified Public Accoutants, *The Auditor's Report—Its Meaning and Significance,* New York, 1967. A useful 22-page booklet, prepared by the National Conference of Bankers and Certified Public Accountants, discussing audit procedures and reports.

Corbin, Donald A., *Accounting and Economic Decisions,* Dodd, Mead, New York, 1964. An interesting new approach to introductory accounting closely related to economic analysis.

Littleton, A. C., *Structure of Accounting Theory,* American Accounting Association, 1953.

Mikesell, R. M., and L. E., Hay, *Governmental Accounting,* Irwin, Homewood, Ill. 1961. A standard work in accounting procedures for various levels of government.

Samuelson, Paul A., *Economics: An Introductory Analysis,* 7th ed., McGraw-Hill, New York, 1967.

Sanders, T. H., H. R. Hatfield, and U. Moore, *Statement of Accounting Principles,* American Institute of Accountants, 1938.

Part IV   Taxes

Internal Revenue Service, *Understanding Taxes,* Publication No. 21, revised annually. Summary of history of income tax and procedures for completing Federal forms for individuals.

Commerce Clearing House, *Master Tax Guide,* Chicago, annually. Summarizes federal income tax information which is shown in detail in their *Standard Tax Reporter.* Ten volumes, looseleaf.

Commerce Clearing House, *Federal Income Tax Course,* Chicago, issued annually. Useful way for students to learn about income tax.

Smith, Barney M., Jr., *Understanding And Using The Federal Income Tax Law,* Irwin, Homewood, Ill. 1967.

Peckman, Joseph A., *Federal Tax Policy,* Brookings Institution, Washington, D. C. 1966.

MAGAZINES

Journal of Accountancy, American Institute of Certified Public Accountants, New York. Published monthly since 1908. Contains articles of interest, opinions of the Accounting Principles Board and results of research activities of this professional organization of Certified Public Accountants. Lists publications available at 666 Fifth Avenue, New York, 10019.

Management Accounting, National Association of Accountants, monthly since 1919. Articles on internal management and cost problems.

Accountant's Digest, Burlington, Vermont, monthly since 1953. Useful as primary reference for published articles.

Journal of Accounting Research, University of Chicago and London School of Economics. Published semiannually since 1963.

The Accounting Review, American Accounting Association, Evanston, Ill. Published quarterly since 1931. Contains articles for practitioners, students, and teachers.

INDEX

Accountants Index, American Institute of Certified Public Accountants, biannually since 1920. 16th supplement for 1963-64. Lists articles by subject, author, and title.

APPENDIX

TABLE A-1
Significant Positions on Cost Curves

Position	Units of Output		Price	Average Cost			Marginal Cost	Total Cost			Total Revenue	Profit or (Loss) TR-TFC
				V*	F†	Full		V*	F†	Full		
A	40	Losing money	$1.10	$.65	$.50	$1.15	$.42	$26.00	$20.00	$46.00	$44.00	$(2.00)
B	43	Break-even point	1.10	.63	.47	1.10	.41	27.30	20.00	47.30	47.30	none
C	50	Lowest marginal cost‡	1.10	.60	.40	1.00	.40	30.00	20.00	50.00	55.00	5.00
D	65	Lowest average variable cost (equals marginal cost)	1.10	.56	.30	.86	.56	36.00	20.00	56.00	71.50	15.50
E	80	Lowest average full cost (equals marginal cost)	1.10	.57	.25	.82	.82	46.00	20.00	66.00	88.00	22.00
F	90	Maximum profit (marginal cost = price)	1.10	.62	.22	.84	1.10	56.00	20.00	76.00	99.00	23.00
G	100	Point beyond maximum profit (marginal cost above price)	1.10	.68	.20	.88	1.35	68.00	20.00	88.00	110.00	22.00

*V = variable.
†F = fixed.
‡Point at which total full cost commences to increase at an increasing rate.

TABLE A-2

"FIFO" and "LIFO" Bases for Determination of Income

(1) Year	(2) Cost Price	(3) Inventory FIFO	(4) LIFO	(5) Sales Price	(6) Receipts	(7) Cost FIFO	(8) Cost LIFO	(9) Gross Income FIFO	(10) Gross Income LIFO	(11) Gross Income Less or (more) LIFO than FIFO
								(6-7)	(6-8)	(9-10)
1	14	$14	$10	$23.30	$233	$136	$140	97	93	4
2	16	16	10	26.60	266	158	160	108	106	2
3	17	17	10	28.30	280	169	170	111	110	1
4	16	16	10	26.60	266	161	160	105	106	(1)
5	14	14	10	23.30	233	142	140	91	93	(2)
6	10	10	10	16.70	167	104	100	63	67	(4)
7	6	6	10	10.00	100	64	60	36	40	(4)
8	4	4	10	6.70	67	42	40	25	27	(2)
9	3	3	10	5.00	50	31	30	19	20	(1)
10	4	4	10	6.70	67	39	40	28	27	1
11	6	6	10	10.00	100	58	60	42	40	2
12	10	10	10	16.70	167	96	100	71	67	4

Total variation during the twelve-year cycle 0

ASSUMPTIONS: Complete 12-year business cycle, 1 unit on hand in opening inventory, 10 units purchased and sold each year and a 40 percent mark on over cost.

TABLE A-3
Depreciation Methods
(Tangible Personal Property)

Year	Straight-Line 10%			200% Declining-Balance 20%			Sum-of-Digits		
	Annual Charge	Cumulative	Balance, End of Year	Annual Charge	Cumulative	Balance, End of Year	Annual Charge	Cumulative	Balance, End of Year
1	$10,000	$ 10,000	$90,000	$20,000	$20,000	$80,000	$18,182	$ 18,182	$81,818
2	10,000	20,000	80,000	16,000	36,000	64,000	16,364	34,546	65,454
3	10,000	30,000	70,000	12,800	48,800	51,200	14,545	49,091	50,909
4	10,000	40,000	60,000	10,240	59,040	40,960	12,727	61,818	38,182
5	10,000	50,000	50,000	8,192	67,232	32,768	10,909	72,727	27,273
6	10,000	60,000	40,000	6,554	73,786	26,214	9,091	81,818	18,182
7	10,000	70,000	30,000	5,243	79,029	20,971	7,273	89,091	10,909
8	10,000	80,000	20,000	4,194	83,223	16,777	5,455	94,546	5,454
9	10,000	90,000	10,000	3,355	86,578	13,222	3,636	98,182	1,818
10	10,000	100,000	0	2,684	89,262	10,538	1,818	100,000	0

ASSUMPTIONS: $137,500 less 20% additional first year depreciation = $110,000.
$100,000 less 10% salvage = $100,000.
10%   200% = 20%.

TABLE A-4
Source and Application of Funds
Data Sheet for Corporate Example 12/31

Assets	196X-1	196X	Change
Current Assets	$ 56,400	$ 66,400	$10,000
Investments			
Investment in subsidiary	3,000	13,000	10,000
Long-Life Assets – Tangible			
Machinery..............	18,000	20,000	2,000
Buildings................	30,000	50,000	20,000
Allowance for depreciation	(14,025)	(18,000)	(3,975)
Land.................	22,000	30,000	8,000
	55,975	82,000	26,025
Long-Life Assets – Intangible			
Organization expenses	3,000	3,000	—
Allowance for amortization	(1,500)	(1,800)	(300)
Goodwill................	10,000	10,000	—
	11,500	11,200	(300)
Other Assets			
Deposits................	400	400	—
	$127,275	$173,000	$45,725
Liabilities and Net Worth			
Current Liabilities............	$ 27,600	$ 27,600	—
Bonds Payable..............	50,000	100,000	50,000
Less current portion	5,000	10,000	(5,000)
	45,000	90,000	45,000
Other Liabilities.............	175	—	(175)
Owner's Equity	54,500	55,400	900
	54,675	55,400	725
	$127,275	$173,000	$45,725
Working Capital			
Current assets............	$ 56,400	$ 66,400	$10,000
Current liabilities..........	27,600	27,600	—
	$ 28,800	$ 38,800	$10,000

TABLE A-5
Cityville, U.S.A.
Position Statement of All Funds—Detail of Each Fund
(As at June 30, 196X–1)

Assets	Total	General Fund	Special Assessment Fund	Trust Fund	Property Fund
Current Assets					
Cash in bank	$114,950	$110,950		$ 4,000	
Cash on hand	500	500			
Taxes receivable . . .	30,000	30,000			
Interest receivable . .	550	550			
Materials and supplies	10,000	10,000			
Subtotal	156,000	152,000		4,000	
Investments—at cost .	55,000			55,000	
(market value $61,280)					
Long-Life Assets					
Special assessments receivable	59,000				59,000
Equipment (at cost).	71,000				71,000
Buildings (at cost) . .	20,000				20,000
Subtotal	150,000				150,000
Other Assets					
Amounts available and to be provided for retirement of bonds and interest.					
Subtotal					
Total Assets	$361,000	$152,000		59,000	

TABLE A-6
Cityville, U.S.A.
Comparative-Position Statements—All Funds

Assets	6/30/6X-1	6/30/6X	Increase (Decrease)
Current Assets			
Cash in bank	$114,950	$171,000	$ 56,050
Cash on hand	500	500	
Taxes receivable	30,000	40,000	10,000
Interest receivable	550	550	
Materials and supplies	10,000	12,000	2,000
Subtotal	156,000	224,050	68,050
Investments (at cost)	55,000	64,800	9,800
Long-Term Assets			
Special-assessments receivable		90,000	90,000
Equipment	59,000	59,000	
Buildings	71,000	171,000	100,000
Land	20,000	20,000	
Subtotal	205,000	404,800	199,800
Other Assets			
Amounts available and to be provided for interest and retirement of bonds			
Total	$361,000	$766,850	$405,850

Liabilities	6/30/6X-1	6/30/6X	Increase (Decrease)
Current Liabilities			
Accounts payable	$ 80,000	$100,000	$ 20,000
Interest payable		400	400
Contracts payable		8,500	8,500
Retained percentage			
Subtotal	80,000	108,900	28,900
Long-Term Liabilities			
Bonds payable		191,000	191,000
Interest payable—future years		38,000	38,000
Subtotal		229,000	229,000
Reserves			
Encumbrances	40,000	57,450	17,450
Retirement of sinking-fund bonds		10,400	10,400
Appropriations—unencumbered balance		5,000	5,000
Subtotal	40,000	72,850	32,850
Fund Balances			
Unappropriated surplus	32,000	46,950	14,950
Unappropriated surplus—interest		150	150
Trust principal	58,000	58,000	
Trust income	1,000	1,000	
Property	150,000	250,000	100,000
Subtotal	241,000	356,100	115,100
Total	$361,000	$766,850	$405,850

INDEX

Index